The Logic of
HEAVEN

by

Stephen Ford-Williams

Dedication

I dedicate this book to both my Mother and Father who I feel sure are in their Subatomic Soul Cells. But mostly to my father whose passing had such a profound effect on me. This drove me to look for the solution on which this book is based.

Rest with God.

Contents

Introduction

This book is the result of what I can only describe as a dream, which was stimulated by a most incredible deep and desperate feeling of grief after my father died that somehow opened a dream state portal, which took me on a non-physical non-earthly or spiritual voyage of enlightenment, which fully demonstrated what happens after death. That provided a clear explanation to the essence of life itself. Throughout my life - from about the age of thirteen - I pondered what happened when we died. Never did I imagine that I would conceive an alternative solution to that of the religious teachings and that it would be such an incredible journey.

You must now be prepared to open your mind to things that may seem at this present time unlikely, or even a little fantastic. Although this is a hypothetical theory, based on the dream and years of reasoning, it is also plausible that it will one day be discovered that it fits within the physical structure of sub-atomic matter and that its structure conforms to deep within the realms of nature itself. Perhaps this theory could be compared to when man was first told another incredible theory; that the world was not flat, that it was in fact round like an orange. Imagine those early skeptics of that fantastic new theory.

Try to imagine how difficult that was for them to comprehend the principle of the world being round, the fact that the people on the bottom didn't fall off into space. But it eventually became accepted. So now you find yourself in the same situation as those early skeptics of that particular and equally unbelievable principle at that point in time. The same thing now applies to my concept, and for the same reason that the Australians don't fall off into space, or live upside down, I hope to convince you that there is a logical process to the existence of the logic of "heaven" or what we could conceive as a final location for "our being", that part of us which continues after the demise of our body. I hope that you will accept that there is a place where our souls could conceivably reside in the afterlife. I believe it is all because of the forces of nature, and the continuation life energy cycle process, that there is a logical and biological explanation. That it is a wondrous thing. I hope over the course of this book to convince you that this is a practical and plausible explanation. I am proposing a completely new and exciting theory, that of the Subatomic Soul Cell system. The implications of finding the location of a logical heaven would ultimately change our whole attitude to the life and death process and even the way we live.

Most if not all things in life do have logical explanations. However, the logic of death has so far eluded us for a very long time; I feel this needs to be addressed. Every day we are discovering logical explanations for many of the life processes, how our body is constructed by our DNA, which up until not too many years ago was another equally unbelievable process of the life cycle, but we have yet to explain the process of death and what happens next. This ultimately affects all mankind. I constantly ask myself whether the answer should be sought, or whether we are better off not knowing the true function of this process. However, it is man's nature to seek an explanation and to want answers.

I would like you to consider these questions:

1) At the moment of conception the life force is created, a unique energy which powers that new person's existence; where is that energy and where does it come from?

2) At the point of death, what leaves the body?

Let us consider this life force, also referred to as the "soul". This term has been used as a spiritual or religious description for thousands of years, and yet it has never been defined in precise or tangible terms; it has never been examined, seen, or its existence proven. When I refer to "the soul" I am describing that part of us which contains the "life force" which I'm sure you will agree must be within us. I will describe the structure and function of this device from conception through to death and beyond. I hope you will also come to agree that it is an intriguing theory that came from that vivid dream, which I will refer to throughout this book.

To help you get to grips with this new concept you will first need to consider the concepts of size and space. Try to imagine an atom, not as an infinitesimally small particle, but as something that within its space is massive. I will try to enlighten you about the "inner-verse" where I believe the answers lie, but try to imagine the inner-verse as if you were looking out into the vast space of the universe, both having hidden depths and both containing secrets and ultimately answers. We will need to explore the vast spaces of the inner-verse, those spaces which are contained within the fabric of us all and in fact in all matter, where I am convinced the answer to the location of that place we call "heaven" truly exists. I also ask you to have in mind the nature of "energy" and its properties as the motive force which is within each and every one of us, that powers our body from conception through to death at which point it leaves our body.

The contents of this book, and the structure of my theory will I hope give you an interesting insight in to some unique possibilities to consider. I will cover many of the oldest mysteries of life itself and provide answers to ancient questions. These are just my personal hypotheses and reflections on life as was given to me in my dream and after almost twenty five years of searching for the logic to death. It is not my intention to try and convert you, or preach to you, but merely to share with you a possible alternative explanation as to the mysteries of life and death without religion. I sincerely hope it will give you plenty of food for thought, and that you may develop my theory to create your own meaningful understanding of the death processes that awaits us all in time.

1. Who am I?

I am just an ordinary person with no academic qualifications and two established learning disabilities. I am both dyslectic and to a certain degree, a sufferer of dyspraxia. Dyslexia for anyone who doesn't fully understand the implications of it is a real curse, a living nightmare for the sufferer. It certainly affects the quality of your life. It's probably one of the most frustrating non life threatening afflictions. It's like living in a prison cell, where your jailer does not understand you. You know what you want to say, but the connection to the words of communication just don't have the same connective meanings when you want to put them down on paper, and yet you know that you are not stupid, but you are regarded as such by your peers and even until recent years by your educators. My dyslexia was so severe I had almost total word blindness. To demonstrate what I mean, my eyes would for example see the word "the" but my brain would read it as "and" and vice-versa, and that would apply to lots of words consistently, so trying to construct sentences at school was almost impossible and painfully slow going.

This went on until an age of about twenty, and even then trying to form sentences with grammar and punctuation was a minefield. I would have the knowledge to write articles for various magazines which would make complete sense to me, but to anyone else it would just be gobbledygook, and so I relied on my partners to help me to complete these articles before submitting them for publication.

To resolve this problem required effectively rewiring my brain (once I knew what the problem was) metaphorically speaking. It was an incredibly hard process which has been ongoing throughout my life, and yet despite it I have been relatively successful and have had an amazing, and adventurous life.

But then none of this would have been possible without the intervention into my life by a man who completely turned it all around, when he introduced the term "Dyslexia" to me, and gave me the keys to that prison cell door that I had existed in for almost two decades! I will come back to this later.

Dyspraxia affects different people differently, but it is common for people with dyslexia to have some form of dyspraxia, which manifests in very many different ways. For me it was a whole different kettle of fish, and in many ways. If I can use the prison cell analogy again, just imagine being in that same cell, where you are not only unable to communicate with your warder or cell mates, but this time everything you say, and even your body language and gestures, actually puts their backs up, when in fact all you want to do is fit in. And what's more you have absolutely no idea that you are doing it. It's worse than a nightmare when you realize that throughout your life you have lost friends and loved ones because of it.

These afflictions have made my life very difficult-at times. I feel that as a result of the above I am someone-whose life's path has given him the opportunity and the ability to look at things from a totally different prospective to most other people. Whether my theory regarding life and death is completely right or completely wrong, or somewhere in between, is at the moment not so important. Just being able to think outside of the box and to conceive the possibilities of a process that in principle could work, because it is within the cycles of life and death, and that it fits into many of the established known facts of nature, is enough to make it worthy of further consideration.

This presently unknown process gives plausible explanations, bearing in mind that in this universe almost anything is in fact possible. I am someone who has lived life to the best of his limited ability and financial circumstances, a man who has often lived life on the edge, and because of that I have come close to death on a number of occasions during my career as an adventure cameraman. These several extreme episodes in my life have provoked a deep need for an understanding of what are the processes that are experienced during near death experiences (NDE) and the death process and beyond. I am also someone whose mind for a number of different reasons has been opened from a very early age, and opened enough to be able to consider and ponder many of the mysteries and so far unanswered questions of this universe, all of its wonders and yet amazing possibilities that could explain why we are here! However, for this book it is death and beyond that I will attempt to share my philosophies on.

I will start with a background to my life, and the experiences and memories which have influenced the formulation of this theory; the mechanisms that brought me here, and how I came to conceive these incredible possibilities and solutions. From an age of about thirteen, I always felt that I had something important to contribute to the world. For better or worse, here it is. I will add at this point that, despite considerable time researching my theory on the Internet, and reading other books on this subject, I have not come across anything that comes even close to the information that came to me in an incredible dream one night a number of years ago; a dream that started me on this incredible journey of research, discovery and enlightenment. To not only my life but "logical" explanations that have become the basis of this, my theory, and which would develop over almost twenty-five years and form what would eventually lead to the contents of this book.

I was born in April 1957, in the front bedroom of my grandmother's terraced house in Llandaff North,

Cardiff, south Wales, where my parents lived when they were first married in 1949. My father was a man of average height - about 5'10" like myself - but very thin. Unlike myself, he was very fit. I can only remember him being balding; like myself he lost his hair in his forties. He was always smartly presented, which I feel was the conditioning he received during his national service years, when he was in the Royal Artillery. But as he was called-up at the tail-end of the war he fortunately didn't see any active service. At the time I was born he worked as a gardener, and as an assistant part-time grounds keeper at a local bowls green.

People often ask, "What was your earliest memory?" Well, my earliest recollection is of a sound. It sounded like a full platoon of soldiers marching to war, whereas in fact it was the sound of metal rugby boot studs on a cobble stoned road. Two full teams crossing the cobbled road and canal bridge to the rugby ground. My grandmother's house was situated right next door to the Hayley Fields Rugby Club, and it was also the source of the first smell that I can vividly remember, which came from that same direction. It was the very strong and pungent smell of stale Brains Beer.

Living in that house was a veritable smorgasbord of senses, because over the back garden wall of the house was the steam train shunting yards. We could clearly hear and indeed feel the rumble of the trains as they banged into one another to couple and uncouple. The noise of the wheels slipping on the steel tracks as the steam engines would suddenly speed up, with the release of steam and then eventually the wheels would catch up with the engine. And then there was the scream of the whistles announcing their coming and goings. The overwhelming and overpowering sense I most remember was the strong smell of burnt coal, the stench of sulphur in the air as the coal was

19

pre-heated before burning, which at times you could even taste. Then, at night, the orange glow of the fire boxes could be clearly seen as they flickered as they were being stoked to get up steam. These were incredibly powerful memories, and all stored in my brain. How wonderful to be able to recall them on demand.

At that time, I seem to recollect that the street lamps were still gas and I can see in my mind's eye the lamp being lit by a man with a long pole. The house was also still using gas lamps. There was a big old black leaded cooking range in the back room. I can also clearly remember the old tin bath, hung up on the outside wall in the back yard. Once a week it would come off the hook and into the kitchen, set down in front of the range and filled by a steady flow of kettles and saucepans of boiling hot water. One by one we would all take our turn to use the same water, so the one at the end had the colder and not so clean water, which was usually me! My aunt would almost remove the skin off my knees with the scrubbing brush. It all seems so hard looking back, but it wasn't really that bad at the time. Those were indeed the good old days, and they truly where for me.

It is great for me now, to relive all of these incredibly detailed memories, which were tucked away in the depth of my mind, where they have been sitting for over 50 years. Have you ever asked yourself why we remember our past so clearly? Are they really any use, these memories to us? Would we be any worse off without them? Why do we need them? These are all questions that I have pondered. I will, through this book, share a great deal of my own memories, and it continually makes me wonder why do we record and store so much information. Once those times and events have gone, why do we need to keep hold of them? Could there bc a purpose to why we store all of these little chunks of our past? Yes, I believe there is indeed a very important reason why we store all of these memories and emotions, and that reason I will come back to later, because this is one of the core elements of my theory. It is so satisfying to be able to recall them and relive that most basic of human life styles, but rich beyond belief on a personal level.

My parents and I moved out of gran's house when I was three, so you see that they were pretty early and yet so very vivid memories, or were they? Could they be memories that my mind believes were mine? Was the gas lighting my memory or one that I have somehow picked up? I say this because there is also an explanation to these memories that appear to come from other times; sometimes called regressions when used by psychiatrists to take a subject back to a "previous life". And why do our dreams have some reality and others seem so real, yet are often jumbled-up images which have no connection to our own memories? This can be explained by my theory.

My gran was a widow, having lost her husband to TB. She was a small but very strong woman who really struggled as a single mother to bring up my mother and her brother and two sisters. The small three bedroom house was very crowded with my mother's two younger sisters, her brother and my dad all still living there, but the family managed, and were all pretty happy most of the time.

My parents and I eventually moved to a flat in an old Victorian house on the other side of Cardiff, where we stayed for several years, during which time one of my two sisters and my brother were born. The thing I most remember about that house was the shared bathroom. After the tin bath experience it was a pleasure to have a real bath with an old fashion gas boiler to heat the water, even though it made a terrifying noise as the pressure built up, as it was boiling. I'm sure those old boilers must have caused a few fatalities over the years, but for me that bathroom with its extremely colorful leaded glass door and hot water on tap was heaven once a week; the kids these days don't know they are born. So again it was a time which held a lot of vivid memories, and there were three in particular that come to mind. The first of these was when, one day I was playing with my father's gardening fork in the back garden, and somehow I managed to stab it right through my left foot, smack in-between the two largest bones, but it was well and truly through not only the foot but the shoe I was wearing. When my father tried to pull it out, because it had gone through the thick leather sole as well, it would not come out, no matter how hard he tried. So this required a trip to Cardiff infirmary with the fork protruding out of my foot, much to the amusement of everyone in the waiting room, where the jokes came thick and fast:

"Can't see the point of that." "You got the point then."

The pain at the time, I can only imagine now, was pretty severe. It's strange how pain does not get retained in our memories; you can only imagine it to be painful. Anyway, the offending item was duly removed by a doctor and nurse, then, after a tetanus injection, I was allowed to go home. I still have the scar on my left foot.

The second memory from that time is one full of very vivid color and incredibly strong smells. It involved two very dear and sweet old ladies who were always dressed in black and grey, and there always seemed to be lace on their clothes. I'm not sure if they were widows or spinsters, but to me they seemed very old, which in my memory was confirmed by their silver grey hair. They could well have been elderly twins, but the overwhelming sense that I remember was the very strong smell of lavender oil. Now, whenever I smell lavender those two ladies instantly spring into my mind with very fond feelings.

In those days, butterflies seemed to be far more plentiful. The house next door had a beautiful garden, full of superb sweet smelling flowers. Now that's interesting. I can clearly remember those beautiful smelling flowers. I wonder why we can remember a sense like a smell, while a sense like pain is not registered in our memory banks. Anyway, there would be quite literally hundreds of butterflies of several different types in the neighbor's garden.

On one gorgeous sunny afternoon I proceeded on a mission to capture as many of the butterflies as I could and posted them through their letter box. I don't know why I did it. After about one hour, I must have delivered thirty or forty beautifully colored butterflies into the old ladies' highly polished brass letter box which clearly had the word "Letters" cast into the highly polished brass! Not butterflies! I was so deep in concentration performing my mission that I hadn't noticed their return and I was caught red handed by the old ladies, just as I was posting the next victim through the spring-loaded lettcr slot. I felt a strong pain in my ear as it was grabbed by one of my elderly captors. They were initially not amused, but as they opened the large black gloss painted door to their Victorian villa and we entered the hallway, which was dominated by a very grand and highly polished dark wood staircase, first there was a strong smell of bee's wax, which was clearly coming from the staircase and which was now completely covered with the beating wings of a myriad of multicolored butterflies. The air was also full of them. The old ladies just looked at each other and burst into laughter. I was retained by one of the laughing old ladies still holding firmly onto my ear, whilst the other, still laughing, went to fetch my parents. I now started to realize the folly of my ways. I was going to be in big trouble.

My parents arrived with the old lady who was trying to keep a straight face. My parents, who you can imagine were not too pleased at the embarrassment of chasing a great many butterflies around the cavernous house, using my own fishing net, nevertheless eventually managed to collect and set free most of the unwelcome flying intruders. But they both also saw the funny side of it after they had finished. It proved a lucky event for me, as whilst mum and dad were recapturing the butterflies and releasing them back out into the front garden. I was in the parlor with the two old ladies drinking lemonade and eating freshly homemade fruit cake made by one of them.

They were now showing me an old wind-up gramophone which played metal perforated tin discs, which for a five-year-old was magical. I'm pleased to say that this became a regular weekly event as the old ladies took quite a shine to me. I would go into the house and sit on the floor, winding the old gramophone and playing the musical metal records, whilst drinking homemade lemonade and eating their scrumptious cake for hours. They always seemed to enjoy looking after me, which they did on a number of occasions over the following years. If my mother ever needed to leave me for a while, they would be happy to take me in, and every time that magical music machine would be the focus of my attention. Possibly it started my interest in music and technology, and one of my earlier careers as a disc jockey.

My poor old dad had his hands full with me. One of my more embarrassing exploits was when I decided to repaint all the garage doors and back gates in the back lane, with some old black paint which I had found in an unlocked garage. Again I must have been at it for hours because of the sheer number of doors I had given my treatment to. I'm pretty sure I had my rear-end tanned well and truly for that episode, as it took dad several hours and gallons of turps to remove all the paint and return the neighbor's doors to their former glory, under the watchful eyes of the unhappy owners.

I really was a pain in the rear end then. And again the smell of that turps on my father's hands is firmly imbedded in to that memory so much so that I can not only remember the smell of that turps then, but I can also remember having the taste of it, as the air was so thick with it, and as I relay this to you I can almost taste it again. But again no memory of the smacked bottom! The relevance of these memories will become clear as my theory develops.

Eventually my parents had enough points with the local council to enable them to get a brand new council house in Llanisian where we moved to, and where we would stay for several years. But I never forgot those two old ladies, who were so sad when we moved away. I must say that despite not having many friends because of my dyspraxia, I had a reasonably happy childhood whilst living in that council house in the suburbs of Cardiff. However, I found school very difficult, because of my dyslexia, but not realizing it was that in those early years. I was just labeled as a dunce! As much as I tried, and I genuinely wanted to learn, I just found it impossible, unlike the older of my two sisters who really found it a lot easier, and she did very well for herself. It's strange how a brother and sister's learning abilities can be so different. I often wondered if there is a reason for it. How is intelligence passed on from one generation to the next generation, and why do levels of intelligence vary so much from one sibling to another.

Some of my fondest memories of that time were those with my dog, Max, who was bought for me by my grandfather on the same day I was born. Max and I quite literary grew up together, and he never left my side, apart from when I went to school. Max was a

Welsh Springer spaniel, brown and white. During the bad winter of 1963 when we had a lot of snow, and even ice on the inside of our bedroom windows, I would wake up each morning to go down and get the milk bottle in which the milk had frozen and expanded and pushed the bottle top off the bottle on a tube of ice, which I was able to lick like an ice cream treat first thing each morning. Max's fur would be a great snowball making machine as he followed me through the deep snow, the balls would form on his underside fur. And I'm talking good size ammunition, which made Max an asset in the snowball wars on the waste ground. One thing about those days - we had real winters and great summers.

Winter or summer the waste ground was an endless source of tremendous fun, and adventure. I was a master den builder spending hours digging a hole and building up the sods of turfs and then covering it with poles and corrugated sheets of tin. I even had my first sexual foray with the opposite sex at the age of nine, with a thirteen-year-old girl, in one of these dug-out dens. It was only heavy petting but very exciting and scary for a nine-year-old, which sadly set me back years with girls. It wouldn't be until I was seventeen, that I would even have a real girlfriend. It never ceases to amaze me how much detailed information our minds are able to retain. It would be a terrible waste if all these memories died with us.

So I ask you to consider whether our memories die with us or is there something that happens at the point of death that could confirm that we take our memories with us to the afterlife? Again this will be explained as I unfold my theory.

2. Indian Inspiration

I always felt different from my friends, never totally in sync with my peers. I'm not sure if that is relevant, but as an individual I have always been different; for why; I cannot explain. Other than the dyspraxia. I would like to think it attributed to or explained my inability to interact well with my ex-wives and subsequent partners, a fact which has only just become clear to me whilst I am in India, and finally getting stuck in to writing this book, I think it is all relevant as it is all part of who I am, and maybe why I have been able to conceive my theory.

I must admit my obsession for finding answers to all of the unexplained questions about death has cast a bit of a shadow over my life. All of this has made me realize many of my own failings in my personal relationships. It's strange and always a bit of a cliché when you hear someone say "I went to India to find myself". Well I feel I came to India to write this book, but in the process, India helped me realize who I am! Which has not all been good, to be confronted by the truth. I am not at all a spiritual or even a religious man. India's paradoxes in religion, especially in Goa where this book has mostly been written, have made me consider this side of life and has opened my thoughts further to the issue of religion, and made me more aware of the fragility of the human race as a species. And that fragility is provoking man to put a great deal into something to reassure himself, and that something happens to be religion. I think this is because of the strong fear of not knowing what awaits him or her in the afterlife, and possibly, like myself, most people are concerned with not truly knowing what death involves. Personally, I think that the faith they put into religion is so totally misplaced that it borders on being ridiculous sometimes.

In Goa the general population is very poor. They struggle to scrape a living, unless they are involved in the tourist industries. The migrant workers who come to Goa to do the more demeaned work are possibly amongst some of the poorest people on the planet, and yet in Goa you can't turn a corner without seeing a beautiful church or ornate temple. There are hundreds of them; they are quite literally everywhere. These are impressive and quite often massive structures, because religion gives them hope of a better afterlife, and also a structure to their existence on Earth. And unlike many places the churches in Goa have constantly overflowing congregations, where part of the congregation has to stand outside on the street to listen to the sermons from inside. It seems to me the harder the life on this earth the harder man strives for something better in the next life. Which I suppose is understandable, otherwise what is the point to our lives?

Well I hope to convince you that there is a purpose and a reason why we are all here, and it is most definitely not to worship wooden idols in golden structures, where they offer a promise of a place in the next life where things will be better than in this life. If the money and effort that they put into those churches and temples had been put into organizing their own lives, they would have been better off in this life.

Sorry I have gone off on a bit of a tangent there. But although I would never actually interfere with someone else's beliefs, I have never been able to accept the control that religion has over men and women, who give their time and money for the possibility of a better afterlife. And especially those who commit such atrocities as the suicide bombers who kill countless innocent victims for the promise of dozens of virgins in the afterlife. How can that be right? No it is not. That's admittedly an extreme example, but on all levels the promises of religion are illogical. Surely everyone should be entitled to the same afterlife and that it is not based on what you have given to a church or religion. Because some people have more to give, does that make them more deserving of a better afterlife, just because they had been given, through the accident of birth, a situation that allowed them to be more generous? Whereas the man who has to work hard to keep his family, has neither the time nor the money to give to a church or temple Is he any less deserving of a good afterlife? No, the afterlife is an equalizer of all, or is it? Because my logical theory offers an explanation that makes complete sense.

So there, I have established straight away that I am not at all religious and that my theory has absolutely no religious basis. I would go so far as to say it is because of all of the often corrupt and distorted controls of some religions that it has in fact stimulated me to look for alternative solutions and answers. I will come back to this later in the book.

3. Death at the Door

I was the oldest of four children. I had one brother and two sisters. My parents were reasonably happy and they gave us the best childhood, within their financial means. When I was about nine my mother who, like her mum, was a short but very strong woman, had the first of three brain tumors. So the burden of the family fell squarely on my father's shoulders. He had to work, as well as looking after me, my brother, my two sisters and my mother, all of which he did extremely well. My mother's eventual recovery was nothing short of miraculous, from her first open skull brain surgery. At that time I was being prepared by my father, that mum might not make it; that she could die, because in the sixties this operation had a very low success rate. In fact the other woman in my mother's ward, who had the same operation, all died on the operating table or shortly afterwards.

During this time my mother's sisters and our neighbors would help look after us kids, when dad went to work. At that time dad had a very old Bantam motorbike which he used to go to work on, and to visit mum every single day in hospital, which was quite a distance away. It can't have been easy for him, but he just got on with it all.

Mother continued to amaze us, well into her seventies, as she would recover each time from her brain surgeries, the later ones, via keyhole surgery, through the nose. Advancements in medical sciences never cease to amaze me. She was always there for us, an incredibly strong woman, but it was dad who was the kingpin of the family. As well as my mother's brain tumors the family had the near loss of my brother who was playing out in the street one day and was run over by a neighbor's son's motorbike. He shouldn't have been driving the bike because he only had the use of one arm as the other arm had been affected by polio. My brother was about five or six at the time and the family was convinced we would lose him as the accident was very bad. He spent the next thirteen weeks in hospital with several broken bones, and at the beginning it was very much touch and go. Again dad would confide in me and say that "We might lose your brother". Death seemed to keep knocking at our door. But as mum held on to life, so too did my brother and he amazed us all and made a full recovery.

Then, when I was thirteen, my family had a massive upheaval when, as the result of my father's promotion, we were moved from Cardiff to Birmingham. To demonstrate the useless bit of information that our minds hold, I can clearly remember that on the journey up to Birmingham we stopped at one of the new motorway service stations and I went to the toilet and was confused by what greeted me. I was convinced that the men were peeing into the hand basins. Of course they were using the new type of men's urinals. But I remember thinking what a strange place I was going to. It was very unsettling for a thirteen-year-old in the mid-sixties. But again, why and what could possibly be the use of storing such useless information as the type of urinals? It really is quite amusing as to the scope of our recollections.

4. Search for Answers

I didn't settle in school in Birmingham. I really struggled to fit in, and was a big disappointment to the sports teacher, who was very much into rugby and expected a new boy from Cardiff to be a great player to complement his team. Sadly he was let down and I was made to look very foolish. My rugby boots were so old they were made out of old brown leather with old metal studs. Everyone else had nice new plastic boots with rubber studs. This and other disappointments caused me to leave school at the age of sixteen, prior to my final exam year. School and I never did get on, and it would be a number of years, before I would fully realize the reason why that was. I couldn't wait to leave school. I think this was the result of having moved schools several times over the years due to dad's job, and never quite fitting in with my classmates.

Father worked for the Prudential Insurance Company: "The man from the Pru" as he liked to be known. He played a big part in causing me, eventually, to write this book. On leaving school, I worked for a short while as a grease monkey in a local garage, which was in fact an "apprenticeship" that involved more schooling - day release and night school - which again did not fare well with me. After several months of really not being very happy in my work as a trainee mechanic, I decided to leave the garage to look for something else. I managed to find myself a job as a Trainee Cinema Projectionist in the centre of Birmingham which was where I would first start my search for "information" and answers to life and death. The Futurist Cinema was a beautiful old building. I really looked forward to going to work each day, which was so different from the garage job. Although my father was not happy that I had given up the apprenticeship, he would still make me my sandwiches each day, usually sausage and tomato sauce, due to the fact I was on a very low wage of about 30 Shillings as I remember, which was equivalent to £1.50 a week in new money - more good old days! However, I was able to see the films for free. I loved my job and was very happy during this period, despite having very few friends, which I realize now was due to my dyspraxia and my inability to converse normally with my peers. I would always (unintentionally) rub them up the wrong way. So I was a bit of a loaner.

Whilst working at the cinema. I met my first girlfriend, a part time usherette whom I would eventually marry (marrying your first girlfriend is not always a good idea, lads, but we would have thirteen relatively happy years together). But not having a few sexual experiences prior to settling down will put pressures on a relationship that otherwise may have survived. What the cinema job gave me was time to think, and think I did. In those days we worked on the old twenty minute film reel system. So once I had changed a film reel, I had fifteen minutes to wait for the next reel to finish. After having watched the film through the first couple of times, I filled these time slots of fifteen minutes by pondering what life was all about. I even started to read books. Well the Bible to be more precise. I wanted to understand life.

Reading for me was a painfully slow process. The Bible seemed to me to pose more questions than answers. However, that in itself was a mentally stimulating process, even with my very limited educational experience. Almost instantly I was poking holes in this "great book". I remember one thing that with a little bit of research sent me screaming: "How can they tell just part of the story and let people think it's the gospel? and they just get away with it!" An example was Genesis 7:4: "For the seventh day I will cause it to rain upon the Earth and every living thing I will destroy from off the face of the Earth!" This was the great flood, which we were told about in Sunday school. My family was not at all religious but we were regularly sent to Sunday school, and to be fair, I enjoyed it, plus the bonus was that we were able to go on the annual Sunday school outings to the seaside, from which I have wonderful memories of playing in the rock pools of South Wales looking for crabs. Kids just love playing with crabs!

I think the reason us kids were sent to Sunday school was because dad worked hard all week and he loved his Sunday mornings. Reading the Sunday papers and listening to his radiogram. He loved that radiogram that played the old LP Records. It was only a piece of furniture, but the sounds on a Sunday morning that came booming out of it were divine. Dad loved opera, and "Madam Butterfly" would blast out of that walnut case in early stereo. I think the whole street would listen to it as dad always opened all the windows. And then when he had finished the papers, out into the kitchen he would go, and he would start to prepare the Sunday lunch. I can vividly remember now the smell of the cabbage boiling on the stove when we came home from Sunday school, and I now write this with a lump in my throat and a tear in my eye, just recalling those happy days.

My dog Max, my companion from birth, was still alive then. Max was with me for thirteen years, and he waited until I came home from school before he died. It was my first experience of death and it was a very painful one, which I have never truly gotten over. Until I came to India I had never had another dog, and to be honest the dogs we now look after are not "our" dogs; they are street dogs. But they have incredible characters. But when we return to the UK in six months we won't be able to take them with us. So I am trying not to become too attached to them. The loss I felt when Max died probably contributed to my curiosity of death even at the early age of thirteen.

We lived in a small modest house and all the vegetables for those fantastic Sunday lunches were grown either in dad's greenhouse, or in our garden. Dad would come home every day from work and be straight out into the garden, rain or shine. I would try to help him, but I was never quite up to his expectations. He always teased me, as he would say I was a bit of a girlie. In fact he would insist on calling me "Jennifer" because I wasn't into football or cricket. Whereas dad had nearly won a cap for playing football for Cardiff City, but for the fact he was caught smoking in the toilets on final match day, which probably was one of the regrets he took with him to the grave. The other was that he never bought a village post office. He loved working with figures. He could total a column of figures in his head faster than anyone with a calculator. So anyway, Sunday school was for dad to have some quality time to himself before making dinner.

Getting back to the "Bible", when I found out that the great flood that covered the "world" was in fact a small local flood, caused by a prehistoric mud dam which had broken and which flooded the area between two great rivers - the "Tigris" and the "Euphrates" - I was so angry, because at Sunday school the great flood was always used to emphasize the power of God, and if we were ever bad then he would punish us (The fear of God from an early age). And as for good old Noah, he probably only saved a couple of cows and sheep, maybe a camel or two and his chickens. Laughable now perhaps, but when your mind is impressionable you believe all these stories and you picture them in your mind's eye! I think Sunday school had a profound affect on me! It certainly put the fear of God into me at that time and maybe throughout my life!

While working at the cinema I started to experiment with "bending my mind" to the point of being able to have an out-of-body experience, and self imposed trance states which helped to compress time. Why or how I did this I have no idea. Like a lot that has happened in my life, I have no idea why; it has been a path that I have followed, almost without any control. And yes I know it was the sixties and no I was not on drugs. In fact throughout my years I can honestly say I have only once, quite unintentionally, taken a recreational drug, and I have never smoked. But on this one occasion I was at a party in Kensington when I was working for the BBC, and I unknowingly accepted a piece of cake. After a while I felt the effects which was surreal; the party suddenly seemed to be magical and very colorful. I was informed the next day that it was a hash brownie cake. It was quite pleasant I must say. I can almost understand why people take them! But since then I have never taken any form of recreational drug. In fact I don't even drink much either. Some would say I am a bit boring in that area, but I'm happy to just socialize with a glass of coke and getting high on life itself. I still find it hard to believe quite what happened to me when I went into those self-induced trances at the cinema, and now I'm not even sure how I was able to get myself into them. I can clearly remember the feeling of looking down at myself sitting next to the projector, with the feeling of the ceiling pressing against my back. The total experience during that time was very pleasant and so surreal, but very calming on me. It was almost addictive. I would also have very strong impressions of being other people in other times, almost like living in a film, watching it and yet with a strong feeling that I was watching myself. But I did not recognize who I was. One such experience I recall was in the trenches of the First World War (don't ask me how I knew it was the First World War; I just knew that it was), and the distinct feeling of being in the mud and going over the top to be hit by a bullet that would kill me in that life. It was just one of a number of such experiences which I now know to be regressive experiences and many of them were curtailed by the point of death, like being a Red Indian in the Americas and being killed by a fatal arrow wound. Each time the feeling was one of familiarity and connection to the subject of the regression, but always that split-second of fatal pain preceded only by a flash of light and many images and then darkness. This subject is covered in a book by Dr Brian Weiss, a psychiatrist whose book "*Same Soul Many Bodies*" covers a number of case histories of his patients who were regressed through many previous lives that like mine were not restricted to one continent but previous lives which had been scattered all over the world. Makes you wonder if souls get frequent flyer miles, because it is a common factor that under hypnosis the subject will express feelings of being hosted in numerous past lives in many different locations around the world.

How could this be? I hear some of you ask, but I have to be honest with you and say that I still don't know. But I feel that there were strange forces at work within my mind. If I had told anyone of this I perhaps would have been put on medication or even locked up. I know my father, if he knew, would have had me committed. Bless you dad!

I'm convinced that whatever happened during that time probably opened my mind to search for answers, and it was that period that would help me to come up with a logical explanation to many of the unanswered questions, like "Why are we here?" and many others that I will give logical explanations for a little later on. All I have done is applied the basic laws of nature to processes that have remained taboo or just been deemed spiritual. But why shouldn't there be a more basic and logical function of nature, and that is the basis of my theory. Which not only explains what happens with our memories but how we are able to recollect things from times gone by which could not be our own (direct) memories but ones which are somehow linked to our being and which The Subatomic Soul Cell theory will explain.

5. Inner Peace.

Having this theory has given me a great inner peace. To know that there could be a possible purpose to our lives and that there is a continuation after our demise is an incredible prospect. But is it the continuation that we all want. We shall see! Even if my theory is not truly how things really work, just having the thought that it could be is somewhat reassuring in this fragile existence we call life. Just to have some idea as to what could happen when we die. Even if the mechanisms which I have conceived are not totally correct, then I am reasonably certain that the overall function of the theory is.

I hope you will agree, as you read through this book that there are processes required to sustain life, that actually requires what I am proposing, and why shouldn't that process be connected to the continuation of the human existence. Although, there are so many facets to my theory, which in itself is interesting, what has amazed me is that each one of my individual explanations actually works with the others, combining to form the overall concept of the **Subatomic Soul Cell**.

I can remember my deep worry at a very early age, when I had no idea at all about the "afterlife". It was distracting for me, having no idea, other than the thought of the deep darkness of death at the end, or even worse - the possibilities of a Hell. Where would my loved ones go, and eventually where would I go, tormented my young mind for as long as I could remember, and continued throughout my adulthood. This was intensified when I had children and even more after I lost both my parents, because of that dreadful curse to the human race: Cancer. Death, no matter what its cause, is inevitable and that thought was then concentrated once I had children of my own. As any parent, I worried about their safety in their lives and also what would eventually happen to them, which was heightened when my two sons opted to go into the British armed forces. For anyone to have a loved one in a war zone, whether Bosnia or Iraq, when you hear the news on television or the radio that another British soldier has been killed, you go cold. I got to a point every time I heard that terrible phrase where I would have to phone a government military family help line number. I had to give my son's army number, thankfully to hear "No it's not him", but each time you always expect the worst. And each time I would weep because it was therefore someone else's son, brother or father who had died. I just cannot begin to imagine what those poor families felt when they received that dreadful news.

So the possibility of death has played a big part in my life, for one reason or another over the years! So that "not knowing" was for me a perpetual torment! It became more focused by the publishing of a recent book that described many of my own feelings and understandings of the "afterlife". This was a book by Eden Alexander called *"Proof of Heaven"* which although very good, I believe only touches on what could be the full truth of the matter. But the fact it was written by an academic made me realize that my own theory was equally if not more worthy of being published. Sadly I was always told by my children and friends that such a book would make me look foolish, but here was a neurologist relaying an experience that was against the excepted beliefs and yet a spiritual "proof of heaven", without any actual information or "Proof". I feel my explanation is far more logical and clearly describes each process that his "actual" Near Death Experience failed to cover. Whereas, my theory will give explanations of the whole experience Dr Alexander underwent.

It was surprising how "spiritual" his interpretation is, which I found very strange because of the fact that he is an accredited academic. I would have expected him to have applied more reasoning to his experience and to have looked for a more logical explanation, when possibly he may well have come up with something similar or along the lines to my own theory. Mine is more of a common sense approach; a logically based approach that conforms to the laws and cycles of natural forms and the established structures of nature itself. Sadly, I don't have Dr Alexander's tremendous knowledge or education, or his extreme personal experience of the human body that he has gained over his years as a medical neurologist. But he has not had my extreme situations and the vision of the dream which gave me the beginning of the solutions. I do feel my theory supports Dr Alexander's experience. In fact in many ways it fits like a glove to his overall recollections of his near death episode. And between the two theories I hope you will be able to come to your own explanation, especially if like me you have lost someone close and you want some answers as to their possible final destination.

Once you have read my book, you should indeed read "*Proof of Heaven*". I strongly recommend it. But as he is describing his journey, just apply my theory to it and you will be amazed how they run along the same lines. But whereas I gives conclusions to each process, Dr Alexander's book leaves you wondering what it's all about. Because he simply does not know what happened. I will make some comparisons as I describe my theory but only touching on his book as I don't want to spoil it for you. But what becomes clear between the two explanations is that mine is from an observer position, whereas Dr Alexander is a participant. I was looking at the processes that he described. I can explain even those parts of his experience that he cannot explain himself, which will become clear as I explain the process of death in the final stages. There are indeed several stages to death, all of which have the be completed in sequence to the finalization process, that in Dr Alexander's case didn't happen, hence he was able to return to the world of living.

6. Questions to an end

These following twenty questions are probably the most critical questions that man has pondered over the centuries. I know they have provoked my need for further understanding of our existence on this planet, and even what was before. It has intrigued me why they still remain unanswered, and yet, that my theory will give reasonable solutions to them all in one tidy package.

Why are we here?

Where is the Soul?

What is a Soul?

When do we get a Soul?

What is our life force?

Where is that life force?

What happens at the point of death?

What is the white light and the tunnel experience?

Will we see our loved ones again?

Is there a Heaven?

Is there a Hell?

Where is Heaven & Hell?

Is there a purpose to Heaven?

What is the human aura?

How has intelligence advanced?

How do we get child prodigies?

How do clairvoyants receive messages from the departed?

Is there a reincarnation process?

Is there a God and where is this entity?

It has never ceased to amaze me that with all of man's advancements in technology and sciences that these - the prime questions of man's existence - still remain unanswered, or are they being ignored. Until now that is! The subatomic soul theory gives plausible, perhaps surprising solutions, to explain each and every one of these incredible questions in detail, and that is somewhat of a enigma in itself!

7. Getting "it" out of the way

As I have said, whilst writing this book I have had
many comments from friends and family that it may
not be a good idea to publish an unproven theory and
somewhat of a phantasmal explanation because of the
fear that I may be ridiculed and criticized. However,
having had this theory occupying my mind and life
for so many years, it was something I had to get out
of my system and share. I am glad that I have now
published it, which in the end has turned out more of
a hypothetical guide book to Heaven, the Soul and the
Life-Forces that are within us. To many of my readers
the concepts found here, within the pages of this
book, may seem extraordinary, more than a little
crazy even! So be it. I will take it as a compliment as
many of the successful innovators of the past have
been labeled the same. Even Charles Darwin was
considered crazy or a heretic in many quarters. If I am
right and my theory is one day confirmed, then the
implications on the human race would be far more

exciting than even the evolutionary theory process. Just remember that a great deal of my theory covers things which so far don't have any form of explanation in the modern sciences whatsoever. If in your personal search for answers to many of the unexplained principles of the life and death processes, you don't have any clear idea as to your own personal expectations of "Heaven" or your "Soul", I feel confident you will find my theory offers very thought-provoking concepts. But if you merely rely on history's explanations which have been based on religious fears and superstition, then you should also find what I propose very interesting, and hopefully, enlightening. Even a little reassuring that an alternative to what happens after we die exists and it is not spiritual. Although what I am proposing cannot be proven at this time due to the limitations of human technology, neither can it be totally disproven or discredited.

It is my deepest hope that you will indeed embrace this theory and that your mind will welcome some, if not all of the possibilities that it offers. And that you will seriously consider the existence of an actual tangible "Soul Cell" and the exciting possibilities that would enable us to explore and offer solutions to many unexplained life and death phenomena that are still sadly readily accepted without any substantiated explanations.

You may be asking at this point why I would propose a theory which does not conform to the knowledge and principles which could be in fact be covered by the fields of quantum mechanics/physics and science. Well, what I am proposing is so incredibly well positioned within the subatomic substructure, and in fact makes up part of the density of the nucleus, the very heart of the centre of the atom, is either way out of the range of today's technology or it is known but ignored for whatever reason. I believe it will one day be defined as a "Soft Particle" which is so complex/small/hidden/invisible that it has not as yet been located or acknowledged within science. But it is there; I have seen it!

However, I do believe it has been mentioned in the Bible: Second Peter 35 - 8.

For this concealed from them intentionally that the Heaven and Earth of old were in the water having been exhibited by the word of God.

Not totally relevant at this point, but it seems to be the way of the world that if it's in the bible, then it must be true, but I will refer to this passage later.

Just to put it into prospective. Looking for the Soul can be compared with looking out into space, at the precise point of the big bang, but looking for something the size of a pinhead. So if you were to look inwards to that same point in time, within the subatomic structure of matter, which was created at

68

the same time by the big bang, but possibly from something that even existed before that point in time, then what I am proposing is within that matter is the essence of life and, to my mind, possibly even the true location of "God". I can understand this is a lot to take in, but I hope it will become clear as you read on, and as each of the components of my theory are applied to the life-force generation process. More importantly, how they all interweave with each other and in fact begin to substantiate the total story of the "Subatomic Soul Cell Theory".

As I have stated, I am not a religious man. I do however believe in the "creation entity" that we name "God". Although I do not for one minute believe that the God of any of the religions would condone or indorse what goes on in "his name", the countless innocent men, women and children who die or suffer every single day in the name of their God or because of one or other of the "religions". This I feel has more than been demonstrated over recent years by the scandal of one of the biggest religious organizations in the world. I of course refer to that of the Catholic Church, which I feel totally discredits "religion", and this is clearly only the tip of a very large iceberg. So no! Sorry, but religion is not the way and neither are their promises of an after-life! If I have one hope from the reality of my theory, it is that we humans can one day be content with our lives without the influence and control of "religion" and we are then able to live in reasonable harmony and learn to be true to ourselves.

I strongly believe what I have conceived would have the capabilities to achieve this. How long would it take for the human race to come to terms, with the fact we all have a part of God within us, as it is an integral part of the life-force and process-that has created us and perpetuates life within us, and will do for countless generations to come if we don't destroy it. All without the need for worship of "craven images", of "false Gods", for us to achieve a happy after-life. That, to me, is a dead cert. Seriously, can you imagine any Divine Being who was able to create the "Heavens" being so cruel? No! - that sadly is a creation of mankind.

As I have said, it is the possible workings of the" Inner-verse" that place within "Space" where size for us mortals is very difficult to grasp, and which is where I believe the answers to the life death process lay, that for many will be difficult to visualize. For example, our planet Earth spinning in space within the universe is tiny, but to us inhabitants this planet is huge. Within matter the atom seems small but within its space we are looking at respective distances as our solar system, so it has the matrix that will support the basis of my theory.

The other statistic I would like you to consider is that of memory - storage primary for computers but ultimately a bio memory. Over the past ten years we have seen the physical size of storage come down dramatically. For example, a 3GB hard drive five years ago weighed almost 5lbs today you have a 3TB drive weighing just 3 grams, and I feel we are on the verge of bio hard drives which will far out perform solid state drives and will start to make the possibilities of my theory a reality, because the memory storage of our memories within the Subatomic Soul Cell is ultimately the secret to a major part of the life/death cycle. And my theory

But remember, there has to be answers to these questions, so why not my theory? There seems to be little else out there. I believe what I have conceived without the luxury or benefit of a university education is not because of formulas or statistics, it's because of a very strong and wonderful imagination that I have applied to probably the most important questions of all times.

8. Imagination over Knowledge.

"Imagination is more important than knowledge. Knowledge is limited. Imagination encircles the world."   Albert Einstein; 1879 - 1955

For some reason I have been able to conceive this theory. I truly hope Albert is right and that what I imagined via my dream, and will now relay to you, will with the basis of imagination begin to change people's perception of the life and death process in a way that creates something that will benefit mankind.

So if we can try and imagine there is a function deep within the atom, and that its function is there to maintain our life force. It is equivocal that there is something that powers our body and it has to be something somewhere that has not yet been discovered, as it is deep within our very matter - and what better place for it! It is truly extremely deep but

I still cannot understand why it has not been seriously considered before. Let's face it, we know that we must have an energy to power our body and that it must be somewhere within our body. Why do we not have an explanation to this process? Why do we not question this? It's possible, I suppose, what seems logical to me may seem strange to anyone else, but why, because it is the essence of each and every one of us and our existence. It must have a logical process. We are a complex life form but the answer must be within us, and as no other explanation is offered other than the smoke screen of saying "It's our soul". But where is it? And what is it? And hence why I have come up with the **Subatomic Soul Theory**.

Well that's why I have gone to such great efforts, in writing this book, and to share with you the insight that I have had since my dream. What is so exciting is that it actually seems to "work" and explain why we are here, and the energy cycle of the universe which is indeed within us. And it's no crackpot theory, but just good old common logic and an applied imagination.

FACT ONE: Our body needs energy, electricity, life force.

We don't know where it is within our own body! Doesn't that seem strange?

9. The Journey of Discovery

I was a cinema projectionist for only a short while, but quickly moved up through the ranks from being a trainee to 4th, 3rd, and then 2nd projectionist at the age of seventeen. My union representative informed me that I was the youngest second projectionist in the UK and that was partly why he also recommended me to apply to the BBC for one of the coveted positions of "Trainee Production Assistant". These positions were very sought after, as it was a way into the world of Television as a whole, and being trained by the BBC was seen as being the elite of the Film and Television industry.

So I sent off for the application form. I did not think for one minute that I had a cat in hell's chance of getting the position. But I eventually applied, and out of over 1,500 applicants, I was shortlisted to attend an interview at the BBC centre in Portland Place. It was my first visit to London. I was all on my own and the train journey was agony as I wondered what I might be letting myself in for. But I managed to find my way around the city. The tube was a great adventure for the country boy in me.

I eventually located the BBC building, after having walked passed it several times. I was over an hour early but went in to the main reception area where I was shown into a crowded waiting room. I certainly felt way out of my depth. All of the other applicants were wearing university scarves and seemed to be speaking plumbs in their mouths. But I deemed it a valuable experience.

Several went into the interview room before me and each one came out after about twenty minutes looking very pale. In fact one young guy came out deathly white and looked like he was about to throw up. I would be surprised if he didn't when he got outside.

Then it was my turn to go in; I was as nervous as hell as I entered the interview room to find a panel of eight people waiting to grill me from behind a very long desk. They all introduced themselves to me, as if I was going to remember their names. I shook hands with each of them before taking the "interrogation seat" and readying myself to face their barrage of questions.

I soon realized I was sinking fast. Most of the questions I didn't understand, let a alone know the answers to them. However, if I didn't know what they meant, I would ask them to explain. Some of them were very technical questions for me at that time, about the conical shutter and film rates as opposed to TV frame speeds. I really hadn't a clue.

Eventually, they thanked me for coming and then took my photo (apparently so that they could remember who was who, as they were interviewing so many). I left that room convinced I was not going to be one of the chosen twelve to work for the world class pinnacle of television production - the world renowned BBC! And so I found my way back to Euston station and, not having eaten all day, I returned home to Birmingham with the sandwiches Dad had prepared for me still in their Tupperware box because of my nervousness, and my tail well and truly firmly between my legs.

A few days later I received a letter with the very impressive embossed BBC emblem on the envelope. My father was so excited he could barely wait for me to come home from work for me to open the letter. I slowly opened the quality envelope, sure in my heart it was going to be a thank you but no thanks letter. But no! I was being invited to attend a second interview in London. I must say I almost declined, because at that time I hadn't yet finished paying for the last trip to London, bearing in mind I was only on a very small wage even as a second projectionist.

But Dad said, "You're bloody well going to go." He was just so chuffed that I had been shortlisted again, and now to the final twenty-five applicants.

Fortunately this time there was an application form for my travel expenses to London, which included a meal allowance. So down to London I went. I had the second interview, which I was a lot more prepared for, as I had researched all the questions that they had asked me at the first interview. I felt I did really well at this second interview, but I was still asking a lot of questions, and so again returned home not expecting to be chosen.

A few days later the I arrived home from work to find a second BBC envelope awaiting me, this time with a gold BBC emblem on it. Dad was again almost busting at the seams with excitement, wanting to know the outcome. I guess fate moves in mysterious ways!

I gritted my teeth and opened the envelope. Unbelievable! I was being offered one of the placcs, but there were only ten being taken on, as two positions were being made available to a couple of African princes - who I found out later were each being funded by their parents to the tune of £30,000. I don't know how true that was, but the BBC did indicate that's what they invested in us for the training.

I also later discovered that another of the successful candidates was a guy from the Midland's area who was already a semi-professional film maker, My union rep put me in touch with a twenty-year-old chap from Australia named Paul. We met up and decided it would be cost effective to share a flat. We traveled down to London and found flat hunting there an arduous experience, but we managed to find a really nice first floor flat in Ealing, London.

Again my people skills were not good, and poor Paul
had a lot to deal with, I now realize! I so didn't at the
time! Our flat was just a short walk from The Ealing
film studios, where the BBC had its training academy.
Our first day was surreal. Paul and I entered the
hallowed gates of one of the most renowned film
studios in the world, made famous by the Ealing Film
comedies of the 50s & 60s. Paul was a great film buff
and would be like a travel guide. He was great; he
knew everything there was to know, like a talking
encyclopedia of film history! We were given our
introduction speech by one of the heads of Television
who in no uncertain terms told us what an incredible
opportunity we had been given. Which we all knew
only too well. There were guys from all over - from
Ireland, Manchester, and a few from London - which
I felt was strange. I would have thought it would have
been easier for the BBC to get all of the positions
filled by people from the London area, but I was very
glad they didn't.

I must say I was really pleased to have Paul's company. Hc was considerably more world-wise than myself, having moved from Australia and lived in digs since coming to the UK. He had also been working in a cinema in the Midlands, to support himself when he first came to the UK. Secretly, I felt that the BBC had made a big mistake in offering me the position, but nevertheless here I was. After being introduced to some of the training team and the other successful applicants we were given a brief rundown of what would be happening over our training period.

Coffee break came and we were all directed to the BBC Canteen, an institution in its own right. On the way, we found ourselves walking down what must have been a film set, that had a cobbled street (made out of rubber), and which gave us the feeling of being in what we imagined at the time to be a French village. Then as we entered the canteen we were confronted by what seemed like a hundred German soldiers, all in full combat uniform, complete with guns. We were then informed that we had just walked through the set of *Colditz*, a wartime drama which was in full production at that time. We just looked at each other and thought, yes, we have arrived. We were "Working in Television". And this would be the same each day at the different canteens around the BBC - Lime Grove, Broadcasting House, Television Centre. We would have tea with so many different types of characters, including Cyber men from "*Doctor Who*". But my favorite place was the BBC Club at the Television centre, which we were able to enter with our "BBC Identity Card". It was like a dream. The BBC club was where we rubbed shoulders with the cream of British Television. I was even friendly with the girls of "*Pan's People*" from '*Top of the Pops*', which for an impressionable nearly nineteen-year-old was an amazing experience. I have very fond memories of those times at the BBC.

After the equivalent of a technical, army boot camp, which lasted three months, but just flew by, we had the exams to see where in the BBC technical structure they would slot us.

I really struggled with the course and the exams were impossible for me, bearing in mind I had left school before my exam year, making me not at all academic. Most of the information just did not sink in, as hard as I tried, and I had very little comprehension of all the technical data. However, on a practical basis and with common sense, I was fine. Even being asked to do some proper jobs in the field for the BBC at salubrious places around London. Showing programs to government and business VIPs - even ambassadors at their embassies - it was exciting stuff and whenever I had to flash my BBC ID card I felt very special. But I still fully expected to be sent home after the basic training was completed.

After the exams were over, and just before the results were due to be released, I was summoned into see the Head of the BBC Training Unit, Mr. Ron Whatley, a lovely man and so cool. Before he had time to say anything, I quickly asked, "Why did you offer me a position? I do not have the qualifications or abilities of the rest of my peers! "

"Because you were the only one to ask more bloody questions than the interview panel asked you," he told me, "and that you had something different about you. But you do know that you have a problem?""

"Yes I know. I'm thick," I said. "Well that's what my teachers always told me."

"No," he then sharply interrupted me. "You're dyslexic."

I had never heard that term before. However, after explaining it to me, he added, "Some of the greatest minds in history have been dyslexic."

It was as if the top of my head had been opened and the light of the universe poured in.

That moment changed my life. I wasn't thick, but I knew now why I was thought to be thick! I was because I was dyslexic. I was potentially special, which I had always felt. I did not find out I had dyspraxia until much later in life, when one of my nephews was diagnosed with the disorder and when it was explained to me by my sister, it explained a lot of what had gone wrong in my life, especially with my friendships.

Fortunately, I didn't get booted out of the BBC, but I was put into "Preview Projection" at East Tower, Television Centre, White City, London, which was the very bottom rung of the BBC technical services. But I had great access to the BBC Club and in the evenings I could do extra work by going into the Studio and helping with programs like *Top of The Pops*' as a camera cable puller. In fact I still see

87

myself in the audience when they rerun the old programs.

Paul was allocated to an Editing Unit. I knew he would get a good position and he went on to have a very successful career in editing in Television and Film. Sadly, we drifted apart after I got married and despite attempts to contact him he has never got back to me. I can't say I blame him. I really must have been a nightmare for him! Sorry, Paul. I hope now you will understand why.

I did not mind being put in projection. In fact I enjoyed it, as in that line of work I met a lot of TV personalities while working in the preview room, and in the Stiembeck room which is a one on one film viewing machine, where I would sit next to and operate the machine for people like Mike Yarwood when he was working on a new character. It would enable him to go over and over it again and again, I used to be in stitches. On one occasion I even had

Arthur C. Clark in my preview theatre. Boy, did I want to talk to him, but we were the silent back room workers not allowed to approach the celebrities unless they spoke to us first. I was part of the Television production process, and life was very good.

My father was on cloud nine at this time. His son "Worked for the BBC". His friends and work colleagues must have been fed up of hearing about it, I'm sure! Bless you, Dad!

However, two years later, he could not believe it. I was leaving the BBC, well effectively, that is. I was moving across to the Open University on the BBC2 channel, which meant being employed by the Open University and not the BBC. I was a film technician, which involved filming and video editing, which despite my handicap was now the direction I wanted to follow. This move was mainly as the result of getting married to my long term girlfriend, from

Birmingham and after the wedding, she moved to London to live with me.

We moved into to a lovely ground floor flat, with a beautiful English garden, again in the borough of Ealing. I loved it, but sadly she did not. She became very homesick and really wanted me to move back to Birmingham, possibly getting a job at the BBC Pebble Mill studios. But it was during the time of Maggie Thatcher's three day week, and the best opportunity I could get outside of London was at the OU at Milton Keynes, which was very much in its infancy. Plus the job included a three bedroom house from the development corporation. So once again I went through a very tough interview process and again the competition was hard, but fate stepped in again and allowed me to jump ship. But for me it was like jumping onto a luxury liner, heading full steam for a new world of success and fortune, moderately speaking that is.

One of my most embarrassing memories was my leaving party at the BBC. My colleagues had arranged it for the lunch time of the day I was due to leave. Well I can remember going to the BBC club and starting my usual half pint of bitter shandy, and that my friends had never seen me drunk and they were on a mission to rectify that before I departed for Milton Keynes. All I can remember was drinking a couple of glasses which I found out later were 50% vodka shandy, and then being in the toilets on the floor when the Director of Television Operations - the man who had welcomed me to the incredible opportunity of working for the BBC - came in and here I was with my arms around the legs of his pin striped trousers throwing up telling him how sorry I was to leaving the BBC, which I didn't want to do, but because my wife didn't like London I was having to leave. I do believe I was sobbing. He got the nurse to take a look at me because apparently I almost had alcohol poisoning. Anyway, the director made sure I was alright and then arranged for a car to take me home, where my wife was none too pleased as we were moving out the next day, and she was having to do all the packing.

The next day I had a hangover from hell and that's why I only very rarely drink even now, 40 years on.

During these years my interest in the afterlife and death was put on the back burner due to having so much going on in my life and career, but it wouldn't be long until it was brought to the foreground once again!

10. Experiencing the Near Death Experience (first phase of download)

It was during this time at the Open University that I had my first VNDE (Very Near Death Experience) but unlike those who go to the light and have a spiritual experience, I believe, possibly because of my open mind, I had what can only be described as a prelude to that next stage, which I will go into detail in later chapters.

My first wife and I use to travel back to Birmingham most weekends, and at that time I had a little Mini Cooper. On one of these trips I had a car crash, writing off my pride and joy. I was in the car alone when, to avoid a head-on crash with a car that was overtaking at a dangerous point in the road and was heading straight for me on my side of the road, I was forced off the road and into a tree which I hit at about 30-40 mph.

At a point just a split-second before the impact, I felt what I can only describe as an electric shock, which made my entire body tingle. I passed out and felt my memories suddenly going into a rerun. Just as I was accepting this state with a comfortable inevitability there was a flash of white light and almost a reversal of whatever was happening to me. I know this to be an adrenalin rush , but I also believe adrenalin is just one part of the overall effect, and process which I will later cover in this book, as the 'Download Process' - memories flashing past your eyes.......

It was not until some years later I would experience a second and then a third such feeling of various degrees and which have been part of the process starting me on a journey which has been culminated in the publishing of this book. Fortunately I had my seat belt on, a full rally harness, at the time of the crash, and I only suffered some slight bruises and a sprained wrist, but that sensation would haunt me for a very long time. What was it? What did it mean?

For thirteen years my wife and I lived a reasonably happy life in Milton Keynes. We adopted two children and I became Technical Producer/Director of the Open University Production Unit. I also set up a mobile disco company which I did weekends and evenings. When this took off after a while I had several DJs working for me with my equipment. Then I bought a music shop and the money from my enterprises I eventually invested in my own independent TV production company, as well as an equipment hire company. We had a beautiful home, continental holidays and things were very good, apart from me working extremely long hours, which I enjoyed. But it did put pressure on my marriage, plus, I'm ashamed to admit, as a successful Disc Jockey working at the time with top Radio One DJs as the backing/warm up DJ, I had a number of affairs. One girlfriend in particular who I fell in love with, and was tempted to leave my wife for, may have put me on a completely different path. It didn't go that way, but I often wonder what life would have been like if I had gone off with her, especially with what would happen a few years down the line. But that would not have been right for my two youngest children. It really is strange how fate bends and twists throughout our life.

However, the shit really hit the fan at that time when I became the focus of an in-depth income tax investigation which highlighted some anomalies in my "bookkeeping". Maggie Thatcher's government had a witch hunt for small businesses at that time and she employed an army of tax inspectors to hunt out "fiddlers". But my misdemeanor was just one of very bad bookkeeping, so all I had to pay back was a few thousand pounds, barely covering the cost of the three year investigation. But it made that period of my life a living nightmare. When it was all eventually over, we sorted out the tax man and reevaluatcd our lives. My wife then decided that we needed a change, and that she wanted to buy a hotel. And so we put our lovely house and my two businesses on the market and we sold up everything. It sold within weeks to an Asian family who bought it lock, stock and barrel, even our furniture. It all just sailed through as if it was meant to be!

This allowed us to buy a 16th Century Coaching Inn in North Wales, overlooking the sea with mountains to the rear, which sounds idyllic. But it had been very badly rundown over the past three decades. We should have walked away. We didn't.

Sadly, this is where, after a thirteen year marriage and just six months at the hotel, my first wife decided to leave me, taking our two children back to Birmingham, where she really wanted to be all of the time. She always found my entrepreneurial drive a little too much to handle and longed for a more basic home-based relationship, which she seemed to find, and for which I was really happy for her. It was clearly something that was not within me to provide for her. A pattern that would later repeat itself again.

FACT TWO: "Our life flashes past our eyes at the point of death".

11. The Dream

I remained at the Coach Inn for twenty-one years. I almost completely refurbished it several times, but because of its size it was very much like the Forth Road Bridge - as soon as you finish one end, it was back to the beginning to start again. After running the hotel for several months on my own, I met wife number two, who came to the hotel on a weekend break with a girlfriend. I will never forget that night, because I asked her to marry me just ten minutes after meeting her. The bar was always very busy on Friday and Saturday evenings and on the Friday she arrived it was no exception. The only difference was that my bar staff had let me down and I was manning the bar single handed, slowly getting swamped with customers, and there was this attractive woman standing in the hatchway. So every time I went to collect glasses I would have to squeeze past her. As the night went on the bar was getting really busy and she eventually asked me if I needed a hand".

I said, "No thanks." I wasn't about to let a stranger into my till.

But within no time at all it was several deep at the bar. And she asked again saying, "Look, I work behind a bar part-time in Liverpool. I'll be happy to help you."

I was really struggling, so I said, "Okay", and within no time at all we had cleared the backlog, until in the end I was just standing there watching her work, serving and clearing glasses and cleaning the bar. At some point I asked if she could do bookkeeping, whereupon she replied, "Yes, that's what I do for my full-time job in Liverpool, working for an insurance company".

On hearing that I said, "You wouldn't like to marry me, would you?"

With that she replied, "No, you're not my type." Boy would those words come back to haunt me. But she then said, "If you pay me I will come down every weekend and do your books and work at the bar in the evenings for you".

Well she did that for about three weeks after which I had become "her type" and we started a relationship, and after a few more weeks she never really went home. She gave up her job and moved in and helped me run the hotel for the next twenty years.

We suffered very mixed fortunes, between surviving and nearly going bust, due to factors like BSC and Foot and Mouth. Being a rural pub, hotel and nightclub complex, each time these diseases struck, we really suffered very badly, but fortunately I was always able to fall back on my Television Production work to generate needed money to pay the mortgage and the bills, plus have some fun too. The hotel was never short of fun. I always used to joke that one day I would write a book about the goings-on in a country pub/hotel.

One of the funniest things which I can remember was one day I was working in reception, during a quiet afternoon when an American middle-aged couple came in looking for a double room for one night. I had only one room left: the bridle suite. They asked to see the room, before taking it. So I took them up to suite, opened the door and ushered them in. The women went in first, followed by the husband, followed by myself. But suddenly I heard a scuffle on the bed as we all walked into the room. There was a couple completely naked rolling off the bed onto to the floor on the far side of the bed!

The American woman turned on her heel to face me and said with a completely straight face, "Oh no! We don't want to share!" Her husband was transfixed on the body of this beautiful naked young woman and the young man with a very full and impressive erection, who was now pulling the sheet off the bed over him and his new wife who was on the floor under him top to tail. I hadn't realized that one of my staff had let the room an hour before, and the couple were shown the room and took it and were going to come down and check in as soon as they got settled in. But they were in too much of a hurry to consummate the marriage. So the key was still on the board and there was nothing in the bookings book. But you can imagine my embarrassment at having the four people in the same room and two of them being completely naked.

Fortunately everyone saw the funny side of it, but the American man certainly had a story to tell his buddies when he got back to the USA. Unfortunately I didn't have another room for the Americans and they left with a smile. And for the honeymoon couple? Well, I gave them a free meal and a few drinks and we laughed about it until the early hours of the morning, because the American woman was not vexed at all. The young couple were great sports and very fit!!

And they kept coming back every year for several years. But they always made sure they booked-in when they arrived.

It always seemed to happen to Americans. Again, one afternoon I'm on the bar and I had people in the bar so I couldn't show a single gentleman up to see a room. So I asked if he wouldn't mind going up to look at the room on his own, and then come back and let me know if he wanted it. He agreed and took the key.

Five minutes later he returned with a puzzled look on his face. In a real broad American accent, he said at the top of his voice, "Do I have to pay extra for a bed?"

"Sorry?" I queried, puzzled by his question.

"Do I have to pay extra for a bed?" he repeated. "There's no bed in the room!"

Then I realized the maintenance man was redecorating room by room. He should have marked the room out on the chart, but he had forgotten. But by now all the people in the bar were in tears with laughter because, of the embarrassment of the large American gentleman who wanted a bed in his room. As soon as I realized what had happened I offered him another room which he accepted. And again we had a drink and a good laugh later about it.

Around this time to cut the running costs, I changed my heating and cooking gas supplier and was automatically entered into a competition to win a Brand new Land-Rover Discovery, as a new client. All I had to do was answer ten questions and complete a thirty word tie breaker. Which I did and sent off the card in the post after giving it a little kiss for luck and then thought no more about it.

Well what do you know? Again I was working at the bar when the phone rang and a woman at the end of the phone said, "Can I speak to Mr Williams?" I told her she was and she said, "Mr Williams, I have some good news for you."

Now my locals were always playing pranks on me, and I on them, so when the woman on the phone told me I had won the Discovery, I smelt a rat, so I just said, "Oh yes, have I?" So, I think sensing I didn't believe her, she then said, "Just phone this number and we will confirm it."

Well, I couldn't phone out from downstairs; it would have to be done from the office. So I asked my wife who was sitting in the bar with some of the locals if she would just go up to the office and ring this number I'd been given. "They have some news for you," I told her, thinking she was in on the prank. And without questioning me she went up to the office and a few minutes later she came back with a big grin on her face.

"You've won a new Land-Rover Discovery," she said.

I had indeed won this beautiful brand new gleaming white Land-Rover Discovery. Fate had smiled on me again. In fact I won several competitions that year, including a very expensive leather jacket, and a magnum of Champaign. It was a very lucky year for me.

But as quickly as luck came in, it went out. You won't believe how ruthless commercial mortgage companies can be to the hotel trade when times get hard. On three occasions over the twenty-one years I was looking at bankruptcy. On one occasion I had a court hearing to repossess the hotel in the afternoon that day, and in the morning I was in a bit of a state, and so I went out to the back garden with a shovel and started to dig. My mother came out and asked what on earth I was doing. I said, "I am going to dig a lake." In old photos of the hotel there had been a small lake where I was now beginning to dig.

Mum said, "Why are you doing it? There is no way you can win today. You will have to give up the hotel to the mortgage company."

I don't know why I was doing it. I think part of me was hoping to find buried treasure to pay the arrears, but nevertheless here I was digging a lake. After a few hours of hard toil I went in and got ready for the hearing to take the hotel off me. I went to the court and my heart was breaking because I had two families to support and I loved the life at the hotel and I was praying for a miracle. Which I got in the form of an incompetent solicitor who was acting for the mortgage company. He had not brought all of the paperwork to enable the repossession to take place on that day and the judge gave me a month to sort it out. And I did by remortgaging through the brewery. But the following years of my life were financially very hard for me, and emotionally too, as my father was diagnosed with cancer. A few years earlier my mother and father had sold up their home in the Midlands and purchased a retirement home - a completely refurbished beautiful cottage in the village - just one hundred yards from my hotel. So my father's news hit me very hard. I remember clearly the day he came back from the hospital and said, "They have told me I'm going to die....I don't want to die."

What do you say when your father says that to you? I have never felt so useless in my life. There was nothing, nothing I could do for him. After two months and a lot of pain he passed away. And I know I never fully appreciated him until after he had gone. It had the most profound effect on me. It opened my deepest thoughts about life and death and where had he gone.

I was in the house when he died. It seemed at the point that we lost him, a bright star appeared in the roof window above his bed. It seemed to remain there for several days. And even on the night the family drove from North Wales to South Wales for his cremation, that star seemed to stay with us for the whole journey. And as quickly as it appeared it went after his cremation. I'm sure it was a coincidence, as much as I would like to think there to be a connection, I know it is not possible, but at that time you look for any sign, any explanation that will console you, or give you hope that there is a continuation after death. The bureaucracy it took to arrange for Dad's body to be taken from North Wales to Cardiff was almost unbelievable. We had to get the permission off each county and pay a fee before he could take the journey home. But he was taken there in style; his coffin had the Welsh flag draped over it. He would have been proud to know that his last trip through Wales which he loved so much was done in such a way.

However, throughout the following weeks I had a very deep emotional pain because of my loss. I had an overwhelming need to know where my father's presence had gone, and why had he been here. Was it all a waste or was there truly a divine purpose to his short life and painful death at just sixty?

Well, I can't remember quite when, but one night shortly after Dad's passing, I had the most incredible "dream" which was more of a vision of insemination that at the time seemed to last an age. I felt like I had been chosen to relay information about how the life and death process really worked. Although, a lot of what came to me in that dream did not make sense to me, at the time, it would eventually make sense after years. of consideration.

When I woke up in the morning I was convinced I had been asleep for days or weeks and I asked my wife how long I had been asleep. She said about six hours. This was a real Alice in Wonderland moment for me. When I told my wife all about my dream, she said that I should write it all down. So I sat at the desk in my office for several hours and wrote as much

111

about it as I could remember. Writing it all down and filling several A4 sheets of lined paper with the basics of what would become, over twenty five years, my **"Subatomic Soul Cell System Theory"**.

Although at the time I could not fully understand what had come from my dream, my notes remained with me. I kept going over them and over time, little by little, it began to make sense. The difficult part was working out size and the location, although the mechanism of the Subatomic soul seemed to work. What I couldn't get my head around was where was this device. The dream was at first what seemed to be a space trip like many films I had seen, but the journey didn't end. At the beginning of the dream it felt as if I was drowning but I wasn't in water; it was so confusing. I was afraid to take a breath in case I inhaled water but I was not in liquid. It was solid and brownish-black, then without realizing it I was not struggling for air anymore (This was similar to Eden

Alexander's experience). I was in a void. I thought, I am in space - pitch black space - and then as if gazing at Earth for the first time the immense feeling of O My God what I was looking at was a planet in space, a white planet with no seas, no land, no features, just the brilliant whiteness, but it was very strange because it was a planet that had a cord coming from it. And the cord was connected to the beautiful virginal skin which surrounded the planet - I say virginal because that is what came into my mind - I was looking at this from a great distance, but there were no stars in the heavens, only blackness, and the planet with it cord stretched off into the blackness. I was aware that I was not alone, but there was no one there. The overwhelming communication was calm, stay calm and accept this gift because you will see the answer to all your questions.

I thought of only one question. What was this deep dark space of the universe with just a sphere suspended, but not by the cord that was attached to the equator and going off at a right angle? As I drew closer to the planet it got much bigger and had changed colour. It now looked like a translucent soap bubble with all the colors of the rainbow moving around its surface and it had began to open like a flower at one point, splitting open, and presenting the structure of its workings inside. The opening was like a tunnel.

At first it looked like an old fashion gob-stopper with lots of rings or perhaps more like an onion, lots of layers, and the cord was the Shute. There was a contradiction because it was invisible, but it was visible to me. It was incredibly beautiful; not so much color, but just white like nothing I had seen before, because I had the feeling it was pure power or energy, and there was a bright centre almost like looking directly at the sun - you know it is there, but you never quite look directly into it. There was lots of movement; every layer was revolving inside in different directions, very fast but again like, well, I had the feeling of Earth in space. It was spinning fast on its axis and the spinning of these layers seemed to mimic the power of the Earth's spin but within the layers of this now gigantic planet-like thing. From the core, there was an intense light but there was no heat coming from it. There was something far more warming than heat. I can only describe it as a warmth of love that filled every atom within my being, and I am convinced I now know what that light is.

If the centre of the "Subatomic Soul cell" was like a sun, then what came next was the rest of the solar system, but instead of planets there were rings of some kind. They were so densely packed that it almost looked solid, but again they were totally transparent until I looked very closely, then the rings were visible. But what had looked infinitesimally small, dangling in space a short while ago, was now -

well, it's again difficult to explain - it was a "world" and in that world there was life, but not on the surface like our own planet. People here were going on with an existence, completely oblivious to their location within the layer within this planet, and it seemed completely "normal". There was the ground and there was the sky, all within one of the spinning layers of the Subatomic soul cell. Each layer was spinning in a different direction to its neighboring layer. They were not in fact rings; they were orbs within orbs and each layer was made up of three components: the skin or shell, and under that was the area that I felt was the memory bank/storage layer, as it was just pure energy, and light (bio memory pure stored energy). It was bizarre, because there was a very bright spot in one area of what was the sky of one layer, and when I looked closely at the sun there was a hot spot that appeared to be a sun to the inhabitants, but what it was in fact was the bio reader disc, and as it passed over the underside surface of the memory layer and

116

read the stored information, it produced a glowing disc - a sun - and as it moved across the surface it produced day and night within the layer . I could see it reading and glowing and as it moved on, the area which had been read slowly darkened, producing night for the inhabitance within that layer. Then there was what I can only describe as the "heaven" part, where there were people existing in almost a living film or video game state. My impression was that they were just like actors, and I felt the script was provided by the memory banks - random episodes of events from memories and emotions which had been downloaded and stored as each of the previous hosts of that soul cell expired/died. It was not fanciful or magical, but it was peaceful and pleasant, although as well as joy I could sense both sadness and unhappiness, and drama, but there was no pain evident. There almost seemed to be an off center balance to it, and some purpose to it, which would not become evident for a long time.

This incredible journey into the soul cell continued and what I could see was that there were tens of thousands of these rings/orbs, and each one contained a different world, which was made up of the different host's downloaded everything, all those memories which flashed before their hosts' eyes at the point they died and sealed their fate. I was taken down through many layers of the soul cell. It was like flicking channels on a television and each ring had a completely different program. Then I realized that as I came through the rings it felt like I was traveling through time, because the clothes that the characters were wearing signified different periods in time or the history of the Earth. How could this be? Where was all this going on? I found it extremely confusing and yet I was absorbing this tremendous experience and almost overload of information.

Was this heaven? I thought to myself, but where were the angels and the butterflies as described by Eden

Alexander in the his book *"Proof of Heaven"* (My conditioning from Sunday school must still have a slot in my memory bank, because I was trying to reason this but couldn't, it simply came to mind). This was just like looking at almost everyday life, but there was a contentment emanating from each of the layers, one of extreme well being, and it consumed me, to the point of tears. I wanted to cry with happiness, but it was as if my body was disconnected from my emotions. It was very confusing for me. Deep down I knew I was dreaming or I felt I must be and I knew I didn't want to wake up. I wanted to stay in one of these worlds, because I felt I could be happy there.

I stopped for a while in some ancient time which was denoted by my surroundings. It looked like a time BC. I could smell sweet smells, but there seemed to be no pain - just very strong emotions; both happiness and sadness. I was a witness but not a participant.

119

There were people getting on with what appeared to be normal life, with most defiantly a purposeful existence, that appeared to be short stories. And although I wanted to stay there, in my mind something was telling me very firmly that this was not my place; mine will come. Move on.

The rings just went on and on. One minute I was heading towards the core where everything was much brighter and there was a pounding like a heartbeat deep and low, lots of happiness, but then, as if I was dragged by the scruff of my neck, my forward motion was halted. I was being prevented from going forward and felt as though I was being told with great emotion that: "No, you're not ready for that", and I then found myself traveling backwards as if on a train and I was sitting with my back to the engine, so I could once again see where I had been and the light from the centre started to dim. I was passing back through the layers, some in night and some in day, and as I traveled faster the day and night just became a flickering blur. It was strange traveling backwards. Before my speed picked up I could more clearly see, as I punched through the layer of each ring, it had a tough skin or a crust-shell on the outermost surface, and as I passed through that part of the ring, it looked as if the skin had been scorched, by heat or an intense reaction of some kind. I could clearly see that there had been something which had left a deep impression on the skin, but whatever it was, clearly was not there any longer.

Again there was a feeling that whatever it was, it was very important to the process. But why had it gone and what was its purpose? Clearly the process that had removed it was very violent and when I would eventually come to the answer to this enigma it would explain so much of the start of life process. It would amaze me, and I hope it will have the same effect on you, if your mind can visualize the function of this part of the process. Because it is the reason we are all here and why we are who we are. The overwhelming feeling was one of massive size as this was a now appearing to me as the time it took to travel through each layer and then it once again as if it was a planet out in space. I would come to realize that the inner-space of matter was just as big as the universe of space. But here was this planet with an umbilical cord, reaching out into the deep darkness of that space, and I could see there was something running out along the cord from the planet, what looked like sparks or pulses of light with a very bright intensity heading out into the darkness. It all sounds so crazy, now but at the time it all felt that it is the way. As I started to move away from the planet-like object it slowly closed up and the skin was again virginal and intact, totally white except at the point it was connected to the umbilical cord. My journey then soared up, following the cord and the pulsating lights which were going in the same direction as I was traveling, deep into darkness. I can remember looking back at the orb and I felt a great feeling of privilege and enlightenment, but not without a deal of confusion as I think what I was feeling was what the first astronauts must have felt as they took off from the moon, aware that they were leaving it behind them! But my journey was now being dictated by this cord I was following. I was not in any kind of craft or even in a suit; I was just there now traveling at the speed of what must have been my imagination but seemed close to the speed of light, as fast as the pulses which were traveling up the cord. I was catching up with them until we were in complete sync and the pulses seemed to stop!

There was so much more to the dream, all of which will be revealed as we progress. This was the beginning of what was to become a life obsession for me. All of the information was induced into me almost like a teacher telling a class, but without words. I was addressed subconsciously as the "messenger". You are "the messenger", you must inform them! I was not sure who "them" are, but it seemed extremely important that I pass on this information. But I was having difficulty reasoning out what was happening. I was trying to ask questions by projecting them mentally. It wasn't like a normal conversation as I didn't speak the same language. Yet I could understand what they were transmitting to me. It all sounds so crazy I know, and yet this was not just a dream; it was far too vivid and detailed, and with an intensity which was full of emotion and yearnings. It would have been easy to feel it was religious, as our human instincts and upbringing will always revert back to our teachings from when we were young. Anything of this nature - "the unexplainable" - could easily be misconstrued and labelled as religious. But NO, that was defiantly not the case, and that came through powerfully as if I was being scolded by a parent "No!" came the undeniable message. "It is nature." NATURE! Biological! - the essence of life! "Religion is mistaken", or it could have been, "Religion is a MISTAKE!" The messenger was desperate. The phrase was uttered forcibly again and again..

FACT THREE: There must be a life force within us!

12. China: Bullet in the breech

During this year, I had my second VNDE whilst I was filming in China for ITV TransWorld Sport. to try and pay my mortgage on the hotel once again. This time it was for the Paragliding World Cup - an international event that was like the Olympics of the paragliding community. I was fortunate to follow it all around the world from Spain to Australia and here I was in China. I was setting up to film on a railway station platform in the centre of China.

I had sixteen paraglider pilots with their huge paraglider bags of all different vivid colors lined up and waiting for the next train to come into the station. In China at that time, they still had the big beautiful old steam trains, each with a big brass smoke stack and a sturdy black iron cow-catcher on the front. With all that black and brass of the train and the bright red of the Chinese flags which stuck out like porcupine quails, and with the expected rush of steam as the

126

train came into the station, combining with the colors of these huge paraglider bags, it would have been a fantastic shot. We could hear the train in the distance, and the whistle blowing as it was coming around the bend and about to approach the station. Everything was ready.

I had the camera locked off on the tripod, down quite low, a nice wide angle ready for the action, when suddenly there came a lot of screaming and shouting from the other end of the platform. This I tried to completely ignore for the time being; my eye was pressed against the viewfinder of the camera. I was just about the press the record button. Suddenly I became aware that I was completely surrounded by soldiers, and several guns were being pointed directly at me. A very angry red-faced young officer was apparently trying to get my attention, but in my mind the train is coming and I am mentally focused on getting this incredible shot. I was absolutely determined to get what I hoped will be a spectacular title sequence, which I really needed for the start of my program.

The junior officer clearly had other ideas and tapped me very hard on the side of my head with his pistol. He then saw me press the button. I was hoping to just leave the camera running whilst I sorted out this son-of-a-bitch, but as I lifted my head from the camera he angrily knocked the camera off shot and placed the end of the barrel of his gun on to my nose, screaming at me in Chinese as he pushed the barrel even harder into my face. And then he cocked it. Everything seemed to slow down as the hammer was pulled back. I heard the bullet click into the breech and my body went into "shock mode".

I believe when death is imminent the body starts a process, a preparation sequence for the download of all our life's experiences, memories and emotions, and this to my mind explains what happens when people close to sudden death say that their entire life flashed before their eyes. This is very common with people who drown, when the chances of revival are better than in other incidents of near death experiences. I have often puzzled over what happens at times like this. Why should our lives flash before our eyes in this way? Clearly they can't literally flash before our eyes, however obviously our brain thinks the images are passing some point between our eyes and that point of the brain that senses imagery. Anyway, there is something happening with our memories and when you think about it you will not come up with many solutions to this riddle. So applying logic, if the memories are appearing to flash before the eyes or brain they must be going somewhere, so where can that be, and why? And the only plausible explanation is that they are going to be reused, so why and where could they be going? Well the best I could come up with was that it is a "download" preparation for the final point of death, to the completion of the life to death process.

The recollection of survivors of "near death experiences" is that when they are revived they remember that they were aware of their lives flashing past their eyes. It was probably via the synaptic nerve, and that they were on a journey to the light which I saw in my dream. I hope you will agree that something is going on here for which, as yet, there has been no viable explanation.

So if you give me the benefit of the doubt that what is happening is my "download" theory, then we have now started to unfold the beginning of the process to how the Subatomic Soul Cell Theory works.

Memories are, I believe, one of the key components of the Subatomic Soul Process but just one of the vital parts. We spend a lifetime creating memories which we carefully store in the depths of our mind to remain readily available to use. But why? Once we have lived that part of our life why do we need to keep them?

To understand why, we have to look into what a memory is. With only the fairly recent developments of MRI scanners it can now be clearly seen that as the brain works there are small bursts of energy that are associated with thoughts and memories. These are then stored in the brain for whatever reason, whether it is for recall or could there be another and possibly the prime reason? Let's just suppose that at the point of death all our memories are in fact as I say downloaded to our "soul". NDE survivors are convinced that they clearly saw their life's experiences running quickly somewhere. Why? One thing in this universe is certain; energy cannot be destroyed - it merely changes form or state. So just prior to death we have all our memories going somewhere, but why? Now just look at every memory as a little packet of tiny amounts of energy.

Needless to say, I did not get shot dead in China and I didn't get my opening footage either. Apparently in China the "waiting room" is for waiting and the "platform" is for boarding and alighting the train, or if not you will be shot.

My terrifying experience was only a short time after the Tiananmen Square incident, at a time in China when they shot first and then sent a bill for the cost of the bullet to your family. China was and is an amazing place, and I hope to return there one day, but I will never-forget to wait in the waiting room if I travel by train!

Fortunately we were due to leave the country the next day, otherwise, I think I would have been arrested. I think I would have been if it had happened at the start of the trip. We actually had a secret police officer assigned to us for our entire time in China. Funnily, he left us just an hour before the station drama. He was a pain for the entire production. If he didn't want me to take a shot he wouldn't say anything. He would wait until I had set up the shot and just as I was about to start filming he would walk in front of the camera. So it became a game; I would pretend to set a shot in one direction, he would walk into shot and then I would swing the camera around to get the actual shot I wanted. Coincidently this was one of the few productions that my now ex-wife accompanied me on as my PA. She was quite shaken by the station gun incident. She never came again, and she put pressure on me to retire from TV productions.

One thing that kept puzzling me for years after my dream was why were the pulses traveling away from the subatomic soul cell if it was there to receive the download at the point of death. Then, one day several years after the dream, it occurred to me that the soul cell was providing something to its host, and the pulses I was following were the life force being fed to its host. The pulses were energy going up the skin of the umbilical cord which indeed do travel at the speed of light, or so I believe. So now it is starting to fall into place.

When, during the dream, I had caught up with the pulses of light and after my guide had had the insistence moment, the feeling was turned to one of "You must look and observe death at the essence of creation" which at the time seemed to be a contradiction in terms and did not make sense to me for a long while. As I looked back along the cord as the pulses came to a stop, they then changed direction and were now going into the planet (Subatomic Souls Cell). But now, instead of pulses of light, there were images, faces, hundreds of faces and people laughing, crying, playing. It was like flicking through a photo album of moving pictures, and then it got faster and faster until they became a blur and I couldn't recognize anything. But then there was an intense feeling of loss, worry, longing, heartache, and a welling-up of every emotion known to me, almost an explosion of grief of whoever I was allowed to observe had expired, and with that the cord looked like a python that had swallowed a large prey and was moving along the cord and into the orb. Then the cord shuddered and began to twist and seal, forming a breaking point which steadily separated, then thrashing around like a hose pipe under full pressure. But I was mistaken. It was purposeful and the bulge hadn't gone into the soul cell. It was being lasered onto the surface of the soul cell. It laid down an organic barcode that looked like mountain ranges and valleys all over the surface at an incredible speed, and soon it was finished! Then the cord started to aim its laser weapon at the blackness which began to melt and disintegrate around the soul cell. It made me feel sick and the smell was of death and decay; the process was the start of liquefaction.

13. Kilimanjaro: Breakfast with God

During the start of the break-up of my second divorce I decided to take myself out of it and to do something to help others. I signed up to climb Kilimanjaro for charity, for the Fishermen's mission. Which, for me, was one of the most amazing life experiences to undertake at the age of 55. I felt pretty pleased with myself, being the oldest fundraiser of our group to complete the climb to the summit of the highest free standing mountain on Earth, summiting at 8:20 am on 11/10/10.

This involved a ten day trek up the side of an extinct volcano, with an incredible group of people. We would spend all day walking and climbing the rock faces. Sleeping under canvas, and after the first night we were at minus zero temperatures, but it was exhilarating and painful fun. I had no trouble sleeping as I was so completely wasted every night, I was out like a light. But for many, sleeping at high altitude is very difficult and one of the major problems on treks of this kind. If you don't get your sleep it makes it difficult and very dangerous. We traveled across all types of terrain, but every view was wonderfully beautiful. Whilst walking you have plenty of time to think about all kinds of things. With my active mind I would consider all of the questions of my theory. And what are the alternatives if my theory wasn't true? Then what is out there after death?

We would all like to believe in the mythical heaven and being in the afterlife in a perfect environment, but is that really practicable. Where is it? What would be the purpose of such an idyllic afterlife? Surely if one thing is certain everything in this universe has a purpose. What possibly could be the purpose of a dream state Heaven? No, I'm convinced that there is a purpose to us being here on this planet and the purpose is a continuation of our species and everything that we do. Every memory that we make will be used again in the continuation after our death. Being on that mountain was something special for me and although I was with a group I also felt to a certain degree that I was alone within my own space. That it was for a reason and the reason was to defined things within myself and somehow to find answers to the problems which I was having within my life because of the divorce and with the obsession of my theory, and the effects that was having on my life.

By day seven we had reached base camp. We had been walking for five hours. We were given only three hours to rest before we were due to start the summit attempt at midnight. It was going to take us seven hours to reach the crater rim. The reason for the night ascent is that the ground is made of very fine powdered dust and during the day it's like walking on a sand dune; you take two steps forward and one step back. At night, however, due to the extremely low temperatures the ground is frozen solid and this enables you to walk on the surface without sliding back.

Climbing through the night with just headlamps is quite a surreal effect. You walk in a straight line behind your group and all you can see is the back of the fellow in front of you and very little else. I don't know whether it was the extreme altitude or the extreme low temperatures but my mind certainly played some tricks on me. We would stop every hour or so for a break, as the going was getting extremely difficult. I felt such extreme emotions at that time. In the pitch black of night it gives you time to evaluate your life. About 500 meters from the crater rim our leader, a hardened military man, had become very ill with altitude sickness. His eyes were starting to bleed and we were all very concerned for him. It was decided that he would have to turn back to base camp.

You can never tell who will be affected by altitude sickness; even the fittest of men can be affected by it, whereas heavy smokers can sometimes cope better because they are used to having less oxygen in their lungs. Shortly after the leader's misfortune, the trek doctor, another experienced climber, had to drop back down, too. And all the time I was feeling I was going to die, but something just kept pushing me on. Getting up to the crater rim was so extremely painful.

When we arrived at the rim everyone was in a real bad state. It was absolute agony, and we still had another 40 minute climb to the summit. Before setting off we stopped for a hot drink. The porters had carried flasks of hot tea, and as we drank the sun was just coming up, at which point I felt like we were having breakfast with God. The sun broke over the curvature of the Earth with a supreme brilliance. I had never before witnessed such a beautiful sunrise.

From there to the top it was very slow going, one step in front of the other, and every foot step from the crater rim to our goal was as if we were wearing divers' lead boots, because we were breathing just 60% oxygen at minus 18 degrees below freezing. Each breath of ice cold air felt like your lungs were freezing from the inside out. Then I felt a very strong presence of my deceased mother and father, that they were with me up here. My theory can explain this feeling that our departed loved ones are actually always with us. The subatomic souls of the departed are attracted to their relatives and that is what forms the human aura, and the energy given off by the subatomic soul's bio generators is what forms the power given off by the human aura that can be seen as glowing colors by special cameras. I will expand on this later.

It was very emotional for me because I must admit, from the second day of the seven day trek to the top, I was convinced that I would not make it to the top, or even worse, that I could die trying. Several people every year do in fact lose their life attempting this amazing feat of climbing Kilimanjaro. All the remaining team reached the summit and we all had photographs taken at the top of Kilimanjaro. It was an incredible achievement for us all and we certainly made friends for the rest of our lives.

The reality of the soft surface became very clear to us on the way down, as now the sun had risen and the frozen surface which we had walked up on so easily was now very fine white powder, which made the going very slippery and quite treacherous. I think it took us about three hours to get to base camp by which time my feet were bleeding and when I took my boots off I had lost my big toe nail on my right foot. My other foot was in a bad state too. And yet we still had another seven hours trekking down to get to our camp for the night. This proved horrendous. My feet were in a terrible state and terribly painful; I was really struggling. But it is amazing how you can call on your own personal resources to get you through this kind of adversity.

But walking down and climbing over boulders was really challenging, I was walking with two walking poles and when we were about halfway down we came across an old man who was in a terrible state and I felt compelled to give him one of my walking poles. He was very grateful and we continued on down. A female member of our group was taken very ill on the way down (another victim of altitude sickness even while descending) and there was a lot of concern for her. Two of the fittest porters lifted her up and had one of her arms over each of their shoulder and they quite literally ran her off the mountain, in half the time it took the rest of us to get down. I was never so glad as when we eventually arrived at the campsite.

Our 32 porters were amazingly fit young men. They carried the tents, all the food, provisions, water and medical equipment, and even our rucksacks. They were incredible characters. They would carry heavy loads and run past us. Each day we got up, had breakfast and set out. They would pack up camp, pass us and by the time we got to next camp, it would be set up, with a hot three-course meal waiting for us. So without the porters we would not have made it. Or it would have been far more difficult for some of us but I know I would not have achieved it without their help.

My certificate records that I was the 111,500 person to have summited the 20,000 feet peak, the tallest freestanding mountain in the World. That climb will remain with me as one of the most outstanding personal achievements of my life, second only to the births of my four children. I feel the presence that I felt of my parents was not an actual spiritual presence, but part of my theory explains why we feel that our dearly departed are with us. And that's because of the attraction of their soul cells to our own and it will become clearer when I explain the human aura.

Because the subatomic soul is generating energy from the use of our memories in the life force process, and as those memories are used they also emanate signals of pieces of information, and I believe at certain states of our own mind we can become in sync with these events, and it was that I could sense. When I felt that my mother and father were "spiritually" with me, that is the energy that is radiated out is in itself an energy form which transmits out of the subatomic soul cell process. This is also what mediums pick up and which also attributes to our strange dream patterns. Our sub-conscience picks up the transmitted energy and reorganizes it with our own memories, resulting in a jumbled dream process, but having some connection to our own being.

14. Yemen: Out on a limb

It was little bit before my Kilimanjaro trip and those difficult times of my divorce number two, when I experienced the next and final VNDE. It came about while I was working on a BBC Bristol production, as a cameraman in the Yemen. I was standing in for one of my production guru's and personal heroes - film maker Leo Dickinson - to film for him with his wife. It was going to be a paragliding world altitude record attempt by Fiona McCaskil, one of the top woman paraglider pilots at the time who I had met while I was filming the Paragliding World Cup a few months earlier.

The record attempt was to take place in the hills and high altitude of the Yemen. Filming in the Yemen is effectively working in a war zone because it is in a constant state of civil war. I have never in my life seen so many guns. It seemed as if everyone had at least one; many had more!

147

The Yemen was chosen because it rises very quickly up above sea level and the air is extremely clear, with very good up drafts and big thermals off the mountains. Little did we realize how dangerous the flying would be out there.

The fact that the Yemen sit so high above sea level meant we had to acclimatize ourselves to the high altitude and fiercely hot climate very quickly. For me it was a chance of a lifetime to film in such an incredible landscape, and because of the constant conflict there it was going to be a very dangerous and an exciting trip. We would have the constant fear of being taken hostage, as had happened to other less prepared foreigners in recent months prior to our expedition. It was quite an achievement at that time to get all the necessary permissions to film in the open countryside, which required detailed and strict paperwork from several ministries in the Yemen's government - papers which we had to carry with us at all times. We traveled around the country in three 4x4 Toyota Land Cruisers, however we only had one set of paper work (big mistake) so it was necessary to keep all three vehicles together. On one occasion, I was sitting in the back of a Land Cruiser with the camera on my lap, and the rest of the crew and Fiona were in the other two vehicles. I think in a previous life, my driver had been a Formula One racing car driver, because he would always be first to reach each destination way ahead of the rest of the team.

On this one particular day, we were heading deep into a mountain area, and the thing with the Yemen is that every mountain and hilltop is a militarized zone, usually with a hilltop fort or an old broken-down Russian tank perched on the top of it. So these areas are very sensitive and heavily guarded by very rough conscripted mountain freedom fighters. My driver and I arrived first, as usual, but sadly we didn't have the paperwork with us. Then, as we started to go up a steep mountain track, we could see that we had been spotted by the lookout, and they were sending a large military vehicle, heading straight down the track at high speed towards us. Now bear in mind that these men spend sometimes six months in extremely dirty and isolated conditions, with often months of inactivity, so they are ready to seize any chance of engagement, to basically just relieve the boredom. I think it was an old Russian half-track troop carrier with six or seven men, all heavily armed, and with an officer on the topmost position on the vehicle. Within seconds they slewed their vehicle across the track in front of us, blocking our way completely. Two of the freedom fighters, AK47 machine-guns slung across their chests, approached our vehicle looking ready to welcome any opportunity of some action.

I was sat in the back, in the centre of the rear seat, behind the driver, my favored position where I could hold the large and expensive broadcast camera on my lap during off road travel. If anything happens to the camera on these remote productions, it could be a very expensive disaster, so I would nurse it as if it was a new born baby. We had been told not to get into discussions with anyone with guns, as many don't like white Europeans and are happy to shoot first or at least take you hostage, which is quite common in the Yemen. So we were to leave the drivers to do the talking. However, my driver was very young, about twenty years old, and looked even younger. I think he hadn't started to shave yet, but he was very proud of his position as a "driver". In the Yemen, status is everything.

By now the guards were standing at the driver's window shouting loudly. My driver put his window down and told me they were telling us that this road was off limits to non-military traffic and we were to turn around and go back immediately! Well my driver was having none of it. He told them we were very important people and that we had all the necessary papers and permissions. So naturally they wanted to see it. We didn't have it with us, the driver told them, but it was coming.

This, of course, failed to satisfy them and they ordered us to turn back now. My driver and one of the guards were getting into a real pissing competition. Things were rapidly approaching boiling point and I saw the driver's right hand reaching under his seat, where the day before, he had proudly shown me "his gun". We'd had a moment just like in the film 'Jar Head'..... "This is my gun. There are many guns like it, but this is my gun." Well, his gun was a very rusty old 45 pistol (old cowboy type gun), and it would probably have exploded if he tried to fire it, and there he was now reaching for it! OMG!

By now they were screaming at each other. His hand had found the gun, but he was not yet pulling it out. Then the officer on the half-track saw it was going to kick off and he began calling his men back. Thank God! I thought, vastly relieved. But as they were just turning to walk back to their vehicle my driver had to have the last word, didn't he? And with that the nasty one of the two guards turned on his heel and pointed his AK47 automatic machine gun squarely at my driver. He pulled the lever on the side and cocked it, and I thought any minute now a stream of bullets will go through the driver's door through the driver, then the camera and then into me.

Then it's as if the whole world goes into slow motion. I heard the click and deafening burst of fire as several rounds were discharge towards us. And once again I had that electric shock go through every fiber of my body. This sensation must be for a reason! I was bracing myself for the pain - but no, nothing! The bullets went somewhere else! They say you never hear the sound of the shot that kills you. I don't understand how anyone would know that but that's what I have been told.

Fortunately, just as the freedom fighter pulled the trigger, he had dropped the barrel and shot out the front tire, then all the guards rapidly ran and jumped back onto their vehicle and at the same time they were being totally screamed out by their commanding officer. Then as quickly as it came, their vehicle then sped back off up the hill.

My driver had thought better of getting his gun out. I was thanking my lucky stars, because in a gun battle it would have been carnage! I think when the gun went off my driver froze. He didn't expect it to go that far, but he was now going crazy, as he had the strong possibility of losing his prestigious job.

If he wasn't a Formula One racing car driver in a past life, he most certainly was a pit stop mechanic. He was a blur as he changed that tire in record time. Well before the rest of the convoy including his boss had caught up with us. No one was the wiser. I gave my promise not to tell anyone, and at that point we had bonded and I kept that promise until now. I think when you have been that close to death you feel so relieved that you are quite emotional, and if you have shared that experience with someone it is binding, although, I was still more than a little annoyed with him!

But again! I'm left thinking, about that shock sensation I had experienced. What is it all about? So it really started the think process again and that's how it would go on until I started to formulate the solutions to the processes of passing from this world.

The big next question is where does it all go? Could it be to "heaven" or to the "soul" or are they one and the same thing? - and if so, where are they? I believe these memories are important and an essential part of the hereafter and the life force generation process.

From my extraordinary dream I remembered the layers of the subatomic soul cell and each layer was I believe the repository of the download, and the umbilical cord that I saw in the dream is the tunnel that delivers the memories and emotions to the subatomic soul cell. Once they are in there, they are what could be described as the state of "heaven" and each layer of the subatomic soul is a different previous host's heaven. As the soul cells are re-used over and over again. What was confusing me about my dream was why were the pulses going away from the soul cell? If the umbilical cord was for the download of our memories, why should the pulses move away? And it then occurred to me that it worked in both directions. Yes, the core delivered all of our memories and emotions to the Soul cell, but that is only half the story. What I could see pulsating up the cord was the result of the bio-generator function of the soul cell and that is to provide the life force which sustains our being, the energy life force delivered to every cell in our body. How would it work? How would every cell in our body be connected to our soul? Then I remembered my journey as I traveled up the umbilical cord and as my speed matched that of the pulses of light traveling up the cord, I came to a branch - but the branch, as I remember it, was going in the wrong direction. I was also in an area of activity; there were planet-like bodies traveling very fast around my head. I once again looked back, and where I had come from was now like looking once again into the sun, and these bodies above my head were orbiting the point which I had come from.

However, these were not planets orbiting a star; this was far more mechanical. Besides, the bodies were identical in size. I started to feel sick, as I felt like I was in a washing machine. I was thankful to have a point of reference, which was the umbilical cord which instead of splitting off, was in fact being joined by other cords, but before they intersected I felt like I was passing through a membrane because it made me feel as if I was sticky and smelly. It all started to become more biological (again like Eden Alexander's experience), and then almost instantly there were cords coming from every direction, as if I was following a railway, one line which was being joined by converging lines, but all heading in the same direction that I was traveling in. This point confused me for the longest time, as if my traveling from the soul was providing the life force for the body, surely the lines would branch out to deliver that energy to all parts of the body. But no, these lines were going in the opposite direction.

Within the soul cell there was a lot of beautiful colors and softness, glowing, full of wellbeing. Once the soul cell had closed I was in the deep black of space, broken only by the thick fiber of the cord and the pulsating light which eventually became continuous as my speed caught up with it. Now things were changing. The orbs which passed at close proximity were deep reds and blues, very solid colors against the deep black of space, but as I penetrated another barrier which came from out of the darkness, it suddenly changed to a soft glowing dark green, broken now only by hundreds and eventually thousands of cords, which came from every direction and which were combining to form thickening cords which were now running along what appeared to be.......well I can only compare it to an oil pipe line which were all going in the same direction.

All the time I was wanting to go back to one of those layers, one of which appeared to be during the Egyptian period, a time that really interests me. I have been to Egypt on a few holidays, and to find out the secrets of the master masons would have enticed me to stay. Even if there was no way back, I don't think I would have minded. From my brief transition through that individual's heaven I could have been happy to have been trapped there for eternity, or so I thought. But what came out of my reasonings, was that that may not be the case, and that was because the subatomic soul cell never gets any bigger, each time a new layer/download is fed in, it compresses the existing layers in towards the centre. I'm not sure how I know that, it was introduced into my mind, as were so many explanations for the various stages of the process, but the feeling that the layers are pushed in towards the centre was a major part of the process. Again, it would take a few years before the reason for that would become clear to me.

Sadly the production in the Yemen came to a premature end as the result of Fiona having a very bad crash when she was caught by a massive dust devil. She suffered several broken bones, and it was three days before she could be airlifted back to the UK. What we saw in that hospital each day when we visited Fiona was tragic. There would be trolleys of young men in the corridors, all of whom had been shot to death. Their bodies were riddled with bullet holes and their mothers would be standing over them and they would be repeating "Umshalha" (The Will of God) over and over again. How can these people honestly believe their God could possibly want a young life so tragically terminated in this manner?

I also have a tragically funny memory from the Yemen. On our last day there we went to a McDonald's at Sarna and whilst we are there a big white limo pulled up outside and several young men got out of the back, each carrying a rifle or machine-gun. And then the driver gets out with what I can only describe as a weapon that Rambo would use. It had everything on it, including a rocket launcher. They all walked into the restaurant very calmly and they all placed they guns next to the wash basin. In the Yemen the hand washing basin is actually in the restaurant. They washed their hands and proceeded to order their Mac meals. I asked one of the waiters what was going on, and he told us that they were just having a meal and then, because of a dispute over a plot of land, they were going to have a battle with one of their neighbors. It was almost unbelievable. I often wonder how many of them had their last McDonald that night.

And then just down the road there was a funfair and families were happy and enjoying life. The Yemen was a total paradox every day, but life there was so hard and so very tragic. Out in the hills and flatlands it was almost biblical; nothing had changed since the time of Christ. I would dearly love to go back, but it will never happen because the situation there has worsened. However, I was so pleased to have had an opportunity to see it first hand, but I find it difficult to imagine that people are still living and dying like that every day out there.

We all returned safely to the UK and Fiona made a full recovery after several months. But my experience in the Yemen will always stay with me as it was a place of such extremely difficult living conditions and clearly a good recruitment area for Al-Qaeda

FACT FOUR: The human body has an aura.

15. Portugal: Deserted in the air

My second wife and I managed to keep the hotel afloat and having and raising two more children, paying the maintenance on my first family, taking care of my father's affairs and looking after my mother, life was not easy. But again we were reasonably happy, or so I thought. But my traveling and working all over the world, earning money again, put a lot of strain on my second marriage, as it did with the first.

I was filming "The Trans Portugal Hot-air Balloon Race" for Sky Hot-air Balloons. While I was away, my second wife left me too, this time after eleven years. I had just phoned home from Portugal to speak to her. I can remember it clearly. I was at a reception in a beautiful Portuguese castle. A banquet had been laid on in honor of the Hot-air balloonists. It was a spectacular event and I wanted to phone to tell my wife about it, so in-between courses of a superb meal,

I popped out of the marquee to call her. When the phone was answered it was my hotel manager, who informed me that my wife had "left". I said what do you mean - left?

He said, "The furniture removal van left an hour ago. I thought you knew."

I have never felt so sick to my stomach before or since. I had no idea whatsoever that she was so unhappy! Without realizing I was in my own little world of filming, and yes, I was happy, but I had been totally unaware of my wife's needs. I think one of my problems is that I have always been oblivious to the needs of the woman in my life. I was unintentionally very selfish. Yes, I provided a comfortable life style, but I never fully understood the true needs of my partners. And twenty years on, sitting here in a street-side cafe in sunny Goa, India, writing this book, I still don't. Will I ever learn?

Anyway, my second wife had emptied our private flat in the hotel and had simply disappeared. I had no clue where she had gone. I had to leave my production team out in Portugal, and I caught the next plane back to the UK, which seemed the longest journey of my life. My mind was a jumbled mess. What had gone wrong? Had she met someone else? What should I do next? I was in a real state of turmoil, and all I wanted to do was get back to my hotel as quickly as possible.

I tried to contact her, to no avail. She had vanished. I felt sure she had found someone else and gone off with him with my children. When I eventually arrived back at the hotel, I went straight to the flat. It was completely empty, except for a beautiful black painted wooden bird cage, which had been ceremonially smashed to smithereens in the middle of the lounge floor. On top of the broken bits was a note, which read, "The Bird Has Flown". It's very sad when someone has to resort to such dramatics to get your attention. It would take me several weeks to track my wife and two children down. I phoned her parents every day, and they kept telling me they did not know where she was. I was totally heartbroken, because I thought we loved each other. I lost three stone with worry, and trying to keep the hotel and production company afloat on my own. But if I have one quality, it's that I never give up. I survived after my last wife left me and I thought I will again this time, although it was different this time as I really didn't want it to be over. This time it hurt to my soul. I had to find them and try to get them back and I was prepared to do anything to achieve that goal,

I employed a private investigator to find her. All the time she was actually staying with her parents in Liverpool. That perpetual lying was something her parents would never get over. Although I forgave them, our relationship was never the same again; they could never look me in the eye, and it eventually would contribute to the final break up of that marriage some years later, and it would laughably be sighted in my divorce papers as a reason for that divorce, which really summed up the relationship my second wife and I had. The report from the investigator said that they had concerns for the children, and he advised me that I should apply for custody of them. Which I did.

The first time I saw my wife after her disappearance act was just before going into the court hearing. My solicitor said that I had a very good chance of winning because the children had been taken out of a Welsh speaking school, and my wife knew it, so when we saw each other she said that she had made a massive mistake and she was so very sorry. She also said that it wasn't me that was the trouble; it was that she couldn't stand to be at the hotel any longer and she wanted us to buy a house in Liverpool. Bearing in mind I was struggling to keep the hotel afloat at that time, that was hardly a viable proposition. I thought I loved her dearly and I wanted my family back, and I didn't know how. But within several weeks I had purchased a brand new executive style house in Liverpool. In fact it was the show house on a new estate, fully furnished, so we moved in with just suitcases and bedding and everything was already there for us. I would live there Monday to Friday and then Saturday and Sunday back to the hotel. Years later I would find out that she had gone back to Liverpool to be with another man. However, he was married and unavailable to her for the time being, but she alleged she always loved him. Despite us being together for twenty-three years and having two children together she would one day rip my heart out.

I was back and forth doing the 200 miles door to door round trip to the hotel every week. Sadly, I put too much trust in my management team during the week, as I was being robbed blind when my back was turned. So I put the hotel on the market for sale. But as always when you want to sell, the market was very depressed.

During the week, I would work on television production work, having built a purpose-built editing studio in the double integral garage of my new house. I had acquired a substantial contract for the DTI which helped pay all the bills on the hotel and the new house. I even found time to build a 24' x 12' swimming pool for the family with my own hands and with the help of my seven-year-old daughter. Between us we moved four tons of concrete blocks, and I had to fill thirteen 9-ton skips with mud and rocks which I wheel barrowed from the back garden to the front of the house. It never ceased to amaze me how much stuff came out of that hole. Because if you put empty skips into the hole you would only get two or three in it. I have never been shy of hard work, or getting my hands dirty. After eight weeks we had a beautiful swimming pool in the back garden, which I also completely landscaped to provide the feel of a Portuguese villa courtyard, with waterfalls, and a path leading over a bridge which had a stream running under it. And the path led to a log cabin, which was going to be a sauna. But I realized that I could not keep working like this, so I decide to consider diversifying and consolidating my efforts into one new business based in Liverpool.

16. Liverpool: The Nightmare

So when my local dental surgery became available for lease, I agreed to take over the lease with the intention to convert it into a Health and Beauty Clinic. I personally converted the inside of the building, again doing almost all of the alterations needed to transform a very tied dentist surgery into a very swish health and beauty clinic. I even went on a Reiki weekend course so that we could offer it as one of our services in the clinic.

I was quite excited about this new venture. My wife at this stage decided she wanted to do a university degree course, thus adding to my burden. On top of everything, I was now having to look after our two children when she was attending classes and working on her assignments. I even did one of her assignments for her.

However, prior to the planned big opening of the clinic I really needed a break, so we decided to take the family to Tenerife for a week's holiday with friends. We had a smashing time. It was a great holiday, although on our return, as we pulled onto the driveway of our once beautiful house, we were horrified by what greeted us; a sight which sent us cold.

We saw that most of the windows of our lovely house had been boarded up as they had been smashed, as too had been all of the huge panes of the floor to ceiling glass walls of my Studio. The windows of our car were also smashed.

My wife's father was standing at the front door, looking white and he had aged about twenty year since we left for the holiday. He told us that it was a lot worse than this; someone had firebombed our clinic.

This was a total nightmare, but next morning, in light of day and with a company called Rainbow, work began on sorting out everything with the house, which was done in no time at all and all covered by the house insurance.

When I had a closer look at the clinic, I thought with the insurance that we could sort that out too, as it was mainly only the reception area which had been affected by the fire; the rest of the clinic had suffered only smoke and water damage.

Well, the shit just kept coming. The insurance on the clinic was not due to start until the Monday, the day we were going to open it and start trading, and the fire had happened two days before. But I took it all on the chin. I had put £45,000 of borrowed money into the clinic venture, I was not going to walk away. So I worked out I could finish it again with myself doing all the repairs for about £5,000. But sadly, even that wasn't going to work.

I started to clear out the burnt furniture from the reception and as I was working this young lad came to the door and in a very broad Liverpool accent said, "Hey, Mister, doz uze wanna buy a gun?"

"Why would I want to buy a gun?" I asked.

"To get the ones who did dis."

"No I don't want a gun," I told him.

Then he said, "Well, they've got guns."

And it didn't end there. The next morning I received an attention grabber: two 9mm bullets in a matchbox, wrapped in tissue, and put in a jiffy bag, through the post, with the message, "You won't see the next one!"

Well, I got the message. The police said they knew who it was, but there was nothing they could do. Apparently these people gave some drugs to two thirteen-year-old lads for doing all the damage and setting the fire.

175

Anyway, I never did enjoy living in Liverpool. I had moved there to keep my family together. I have a great need to live close to water. I think that's why, even though I couldn't afford the swimming pool at that time, I had to have water near me, and I just did it. It really was too far from the sea for me, living in Liverpool. I really do need to be closer to the sea; it recharges me. I have a great affinity with water which becomes ever more important to me over the years, and so I was happy to move away. But my wife didn't want to go back to the hotel, which would have been the simplest option. So we ended up moving into one of my sister's flats in Tenby, so now we had to put the house up for sale as well. We still had the hotel on the market, so I was understandably a little stretched and distracted from my subatomic soul cell theory book for the next few years, although it was constantly in the back of my mind.

So we all moved to Tenby. The children were enrolled into the local school and I started to look for a house. The good thing was that the family seemed to settle in Tenby very quickly. I was still running back and forth to the hotel, a journey which took me between three to five hours each way, depending on the time of year, but again fate stepped in. One Sunday evening my wife and I went for a stroll around Tenby and we walked up a lane where there are some of the most impressive houses in the area, and I was stopped in my tracks outside one particularly large and very impressive double-fronted property. "That's the house I would like," I said to my wife. It was set back off the road with a long drive, two large palm trees in the centre of a large front lawn which was surrounded by mature trees and bushes, and it was just across the road from the school where we had enrolled the children a few weeks earlier. But alas there was no "For Sale" sign.

But I could not stop thinking about it all that night......
You could say it was the power of suggestion.
Because the next day I went for my early morning
walk around Tenby town, which is a lovely place to
stretch your legs, first thing, and I was doing my
usual sweep by all of the local estate agents, and just
as I stood at the window of the first estate agent's
window a woman was just that very second putting
into the window the details of that very house we had
been standing outside the night before. But as always
is the case when you are seeking a property, the one
you want is always over your budget - and this was
way over our budget.

Undeterred, I went in and asked them to arrange a
viewing, which was organized within ten minutes. At
that time my wife had a part-time book-keeping job
for a local hair dresser, so she was not available
straight away, so I went on my own to check it out.
When I drove up the drive I immediately fell in love

with the place; it felt like home. It had been built in 1933 - not a good year for housing as most of the rooms were very small - but I instantly could see the potential of knocking a few walls down, plus it was set in almost half an acre, with mature gardens front and rear. It even had an orchard with seventeen fruit trees which included peach, cherry, plum, pear and several types of apple. It just had that wow factor, despite the fact that the entire house had been decorated from floor to roof in wood-chip wall paper painted magnolia. But this did not put me off. I had spent the previous twenty-one years working on a 16th century coaching inn. This would be a doddle.

I asked the lady owner, that if we offered the asking price would they be able to take it off the market. Although, first my wife would have to view it. But I just knew she would love it. The viewing was arranged for that evening. We viewed the house together and agreed it was the one we wanted to be the house where our children could grow up and one day grandchildren would visit. It just felt right!

Despite having not yet sold our house or the hotel, and that I was effectively out of work, it nevertheless felt like it was meant to be, and the woman agreed to take it off the market as she said she felt the house was meant for us. I explained that we had two properties to sell, so it would take a little time. But it transpired that they were building a villa in Spain, so were not too desperate to sell in a hurry. And that thing called fate worked its magic again, and within little or no time both our properties had sold and we were moving in.

17. Tenby: Sensing the departed

Those first few years in Tenby were amazing, almost magical. We made some great new friends. I joined the local Rotary Club. These were probably the best years of my life and the family was very happy. Almost straight away I started to rip the house apart, molding it into that family home we wanted.

Within three years, I was President of the Rotary Club. I had taken on the local cinema as a short term business arrangement, which was only supposed to be to keep it going for six months, but it went on for over six years. It was a beautiful old 500 seater two-level single screen proper cinema with a very large screen and the old red crushed velvet tilting seating which had seen better days. In fact the whole building was very run down. But I loved it; it was like going back to my roots.

Over the next six years I slowly tried to improve it on a shoestring budget, by buying and scrounging equipment and bits and pieces from other cinemas which had closed down. I painted the outside myself, and most of the inside. I built a new sweet shop and ticket office, in the old 50s style. It ticked over quite well. We had all the latest films on the release date. When I was working in the cinema I thoroughly enjoyed it. I started live stage shows and we had film premiere nights where the audience would come dressed up in tux and long dresses. It was my little bit of heaven for a while. We even had the "Most Haunted" program come to the cinema one night and I can honestly say that was the spookiest night of my life.

I have always kept an open mind about this sort of thing however, things that went on that night really made me wonder if there could be something to the spirit world. At about 3am the production team and some other people who were the mediums all arrived and there were also the people who were going to be involved in the program's experiments; about fifteen men and woman in total. They were all asked to go into the lower auditorium (the stalls) in pitch darkness and were told to space themselves out. There was to be no talking. I had opted to join them out of interest, and we were all told to sit in complete silence for half an hour.

It truly was pitch black in there; you couldn't see your hand in front of your face. We were each given a pad of paper on a clipboard and a pen. The mediums told us to close our eyes and to try and clear our minds, and over the next thirty minutes we would just sit there and write down or draw whatever came into our minds. Well that was one of the longest thirty minutes ever.

The cinema, although remodeled in 1927 after a fire which had badly damaged most of the main building, was actually much older. It had been the "Community Meeting Rooms" for a considerable time in the late

183

1800s and we had an etching print of when Queen Victoria came to Tenby shortly after Her Prince Albert had died. The main proscenium arch is clearly visible in the drawing above the Queens head and was still intact behind the cinema screen. Even now there is a splendid statue of Prince Albert overlooking Tenby from Castle Hill. Apparently, the couple loved Tenby so much. Thus there was a lot of history to the cinema building, so if anywhere was going to have ghosts or stranded spirits it was going to be the cinema building, which is why the team had chosen it.

After the thirty minutes of darkness a few torches were switched on and we were all called together to discuss what we had each written on the pads. And almost all had the same theme, which was World War II. Someone had drawn a set of sergeant stripes, and another a stick and words to the song "It's a long way to Tipperary". All of which meant nothing to me at the time. But it was interesting that all fifteen had recorded some connections to the War on their papers. But then as I thought about it I was both amazed and a little unsettled by it. Let me explain why.

You can imagine that closing up an old building last thing at night is pretty spooky. There was a very long corridor down the side of the lower auditorium, down to the toilets which I had to go down to lock up. It's strange, but as I used to walk down that long dark corridor I would almost always start to whistle a tune, and amazingly it would quite often be "It's a long way to Tipperary". Coincidence or what? Even as I'm writing this now, the hairs on my neck are standing on end.

During the rest of that "Most Haunted" night, throughout the cinema, there were several similar experiments, and they all had similar outcomes. But the most disturbing was at the top of the stairs there was a foyer which led to the balcony, and it was here that the team decided to hold a séance. A table was set up and several people sat around it and placed their hands down on it. When the main psychic asked for silence and started to ask questions there seemed to be a change in the room. It was already quite cold but there seemed to be a further drop in temperature, and then the table started to vibrate. The psychic, we were told, was picking up a sense of a French spirit from the 30s and as the questions were asked the table moved more violently until a point where the medium said we had to stop. This spirit was not a good spirit. Apparently there was a risk that this unhappy spirit could attach itself to someone at the table and they could be stuck with it. I was watching everything with utter amazement. I focused my gaze on the table to see if any of the participants were moving it, but I saw no evidence of that. Yet I found it very difficult to believe that a spiritual influence could have made the table move. The medium then explained that he felt it was the spirit of a French Soldier who had been killed very young and that he in fact did not except that he was dead. We were urged to leave that area and the psychic did something after we left to help the poor soul. He then came down and said that there was two military spirits in the building - one upstairs and one in the corridor leading to the toilets. He said the one downstairs was content and happy to be here, but the one upstairs was verging on an evil presence and could be dangerous if he had managed to leave with any one of us.

As I say I keep an open mind, but all of what happened that night does not fit into my theory and that worries me. But right up until the day I closed the cinema there was no other incidents, other than that I continued to whistle when locking up the building each night. At the end of the event the main medium and psychic told me that the cinema was one of the most haunted places the team had ever been to, and that they would love to come back at some future date. But sadly the cinema closed and it never happened again.

However, it all came home to me when I returned to the cinema the day after the "Most Haunted" event and mentioned what had happened to one of my staff whose family had been involved with the cinema for several generations. When I described what had happened, especially the bit about writing things down, her face went quite white. She told me that after the war a retired ex-sergeant major had become the manager of the cinema, and she said he always carried his sergeant major's baton with him (a stick) which he controlled the younger members of the audience with very strictly. And allegedly he was always whistling "It's a long way to Tipperary" and other wartime songs. All of which totally blew my mind. Although this stretches my theory, it can give an explanation for this sort of thing. As the sergeant major had been a part of the cinema for a number of years, he would have shed a large amount of his skin cells which would contain passive soul cells which had attached themselves to the fabric of the building. After his death his finalized Subatomic Soul Cells (active and finalized) could have been released into the environment and found their way back to the cinema as they would have been attracted to those attached skin cells, which then emanate energy as the Soul Cell is continually functioning, and as his memories and some of the emotions are reacting within the layer of the soul cell the emissions are continually leaking out into the area around the cinema, which is what we all were picking up. Quite simply the sergeant major was within his soul cell and he must be still whistling it's a long way to Tipperary and that's why we were able to pick up on it. In my dream it seemed as if the memories were set on loops because there seemed to some repeats, but again I'm not sure about that.

18. Passive & Active Soul Cells

I mentioned, in the last chapter, Active & Passive soul cells. OK, it's time to start to explain the Subatomic Soul Cell Theory, and yes there are two distinct soul cells. But more to the point the conclusion I finally came to after years of analyzing my dream was that we don't have just one soul From the dream and my journey from the soul cell it was clear that all the cords I could see coming together were all coming from similar soul cells. In fact my conclusion is that every cell in our body has a subatomic soul cell at the heart of it. So yes, we have not only one soul but hundreds of millions of soul cells which provide the life force within our bodies, and yes, I believe that we have two distinct types of soul cells, namely Active and Passive Soul Cells

Passive soul cells which are not attached to a being. These are souls which have been finalized after the

190

death of their last host. And via cremation or putrefaction have been released to the environment. These passive soul cells are floating free in the air or water around us. Just like pollen, or a more apt analogy is radio waves, because they are more energy than substance, but like pollen from a plant as they are everywhere and waiting for their chance to be selected in the next conception process.

The Active soul cells are ones which are still part of their host and they are providing the life force for their host. That's why in my dream the pulses were traveling away from the soul cell that was the life force. It will become clearer as we go on. As I said, I was only initially supposed to run the cinema for six months or so until the site was going to be redeveloped. But it went on for over six years. However, during this time the Royal Gate House Hotel in Tenby sadly burnt down one night, and although the flames came very close to the cinema, the fire did not penetrate the thick walls. However the heat must have affected the roof of the cinema, as it constantly required work after the fire, mainly because of the water penetration, which kept running through the roof and ceilings and into the main foyer. Every time we had heavy rain, and as much as I tried to stop it, it just kept finding a way in. It got so bad at times we had to completely close the balcony because there would be a waterfall running down the stairs.

This, together with the opening of a new multiplex cinema in Carmarthen, just twenty miles away, finished the cinema's trade for us. So I decided to close it in December 2010 which was a very sad moment for me as I really loved running the cinema and would have liked to have been able to revamp the building. It could have been a beautiful old classic cinema. But it was never going to happen, as I was just keeping it going until the building was going to be redeveloped into a shopping arcade and replacement hotel. In fact as I sit here in India writing this book, I have just been sent an e-mail by a friend which has just informed me that after standing closed for almost two years the cinema is only now finally being pulled down, I'm very sad, but glad I'm not there to see it. I wonder what will happen to those spirits, if indeed they did reside there or could it just be the result of us wanting them to be there. There was a lot which defied explanation during that evening.

19. End of my rope

During the start of my second divorce I had a mental breakdown. Well, it was more of a burnout really, and to be honest I had just come to the end, or so I felt at the time. Throughout the whole of my life, I could never for one minute understand anyone who would want to take their own life. And yet now having been to that point and fortunately survived, I will never think that again, what were they thinking about when they ended it, for me it was in quite a peaceful place in my head. My heart was broken, because I never really wanted the divorce, I did love my wife but no matter how much I tried, I just could not make her happy and could never understand why. I had no idea that she always loved someone else throughout our marriage. So I was at a point in my life where I had done more than most people. I had traveled all over the world with my job and on holidays. I just felt that I was ready to pass on and finally find out whether my theory was in fact right or wrong. So I went out to my workshop and found a rope, and I remember thinking to myself this is a nice rope, it's a real good rope.

When I was a kid I learnt how to make a hangman's noose. I sat down very calmly and fashioned the knot that I had practiced years ago and it turned out perfect first time. My house had a very large wooden staircase, very similar to the one I once covered with beautiful butterflies in the old ladies' house in Cardiff as a child. I tied the rope off on one of the upstairs banisters above the large front hallway. I placed a chair under the rope and adjusted the drop and can also remember being pleased with how it all went together and looked. I was surprisingly calm and almost happy that it was going to be the end of a very unhappy period of my life, but a life which had been very full. I had no inclination whatsoever to write a note; I just wanted it to be done and over with! And I was totally resigned to the fact that it was going to be done now.

I climbed up onto the chair. I had to stretch on tiptoes to reach and get the noose around my neck, I pulled it tight around my neck and just as I was going to kick the chair away, completely at one with my fate, and almost excited to experience what comes next. Just at that very point of no return, my mobile phone in my pocket went off, and I thought bloody hell what am I doing? It was just like waking up. What the hell am I doing! I took the phone out of my pocket and put it to my ear. It was a very close friend calling, and she was almost screaming down the phone: "Where are you? You must come here now"!

I said, "Your timing is spot on."

"What do you mean?" she said.

I said, "I will come over now and explain."

I took the rope off my neck, climbed down, walked across the road to my friend's house, and asked her what it was she wanted so urgently.

She looked bemused. "I don't know," she said sheepishly, "I just felt I had to ring you. I really don't know why."

"I know why," I said. "You just stopped me doing something very foolish." Knowing she wouldn't believe, before explaining the situation further I walked back to my house, untied the rope and took it back to show her. And she kept it in case I considered using it again. It was a real wake up call for me. I know life has so much more to offer, but thinking back to the whole episode, I was amazed how resigned I was to ending my life. Clearly it wasn't meant to be, but I was truly ready. So now when I hear of someone who has taken their own life I don't think how could they do that. I know how easy it is because you are on remote control and it seems the right thing to do at the time. But I was incredibly fortunate that my friend called when she did, and that literally snapped me out of that mind set. As to why my friend contacted me at that precise time will forever remain a mystery to me and her, but I would like to think it was for me to finish this book.

20. Beginning of the End

What brought me to the point of trying to kill myself was a period of total frustration, un-happiness, and bad business decisions. In readiness for the day when the cinema would close, I had to find something to replace that income. In hindsight I would not have done what I did, but the final straw that broke the camel's back of my life in Tenby was when I decided, yet again and now in my fifties, to try to diversify into a new business - one I could run from home as the house had plenty of driveway for what I had in mind.

My daughter was due within the next couple of years to go to university. She had always excelled in school, and there was no question that she would be going to university. Plus I still had two sons in the Armed Forces, who I dearly wanted to come out, as I hated it when they were away overseas, in places like Bosnia and Iraq. I wanted to set up a brand new business that would generate an income to see my daughter through university and offer an opportunity to either one or both of my sons, a business that we could run together. What came about was the biggest mistake of my life, but that's fate for you. I decided to increase my income by setting up a new Stretched Limo business. Not just any limo business; it was going to be the only company to import from the States brand new top of the range limos into the area. My wife and I booked a trip to Las Vegas to go to the "US Limo Show". We had a great time checking out all the newest and most impressive limos in the world, and attending parties laid on by the limo companies. We met some other operators from the UK, and it all seemed to be a very good idea at the time. We thoroughly enjoyed Vegas so much, we were talked into buying a bloody time share out there (Another big mistake. Don't ever buy time share). It turned out to be a property we never got to use!

After several meetings with the limo manufacturers, and a considerable amount of research into which ones would best suit our needs (we even saw crash test footage that convinced us that we had chosen the right ones) we bought what we thought were the best and most impressive limos in the world within our budget, which was our life's savings. We decided on two: a 14 seater Ford Excursion which was for a time the first and largest legal limo in the UK, and a 10 seater Chrysler 300 super stretch (it looked like a baby Bentley stretched). It was stunning, but it turned out to be the catalyst for of my undoing. I also bought a non-stretched version to use as a wedding car which was also stunning, as it was the actual Custom Car "show car" with beautiful 22 inch chrome wheels. It looked a million dollar car. However, it was just too darn powerful. It had a 5.8 V8 Hemi engine which developed 400 brake horsepower. But I really loved that car. Little did I realize the consequence of purchasing it.

We arranged to get all three cars shipped back to the UK and I set about getting the business up and running. First to arrive was the Chrysler 300 stretch. It had been inspected and approved by the DVLA, and my wife and I went down to the south of England to pick it up. It was absolutely stunning in Vanilla White, with large wheels and fully equipped with three flat screen TVs, a sound system which made it a disco on wheels, and an incredible disco light show. We decided to call her "The Lady", and I had to drive it all the way back to Tenby. Wow! She was almost 30 foot' long and when I first got in the driving seat I thought OMG! Can I do this?

Driving it down the side streets to get to the motorway was real scary, but as soon as I was on the motorway I just loved it, and to see the reaction on the faces of passing motorists was amazing. I felt pretty pleased with myself and was confident I had made the right decision. We got it back to Tenby in one piece. We even stopped on the motorway and my wife drove it for a short while.

I started to advertise the new venture and the bookings started to come in. Then we had to go up to Hull to pick up the big one. It had sailed through all the government inspections and was for a while the first and only limo in the UK to legally carry over 8 passengers as it was a 14 seater. We called this one "The Daddy". Again I drove it back, and again it was a stunning machine fully loaded with all the sound and lighting and the big chrome wheels. My fleet was growing and so was the business, but getting the operator's license was proving very difficult. Because I was the first to operate new large legal limos in Wales I wanted a license. But there was no such limo license. You could have a private hire license for up to 8 seats but the was no license for over 8 - and the only way of doing it legally was to register as - wait for it - as a "BUS" company. So I did that through

Vosa which opened a can of worms but I got my license. But then the government soon changed all the rules. During this time my wife and I were trying to promote the business and on a Sunday afternoon shortly after collecting the short version of the Chrysler 300, the jewel of my fleet, we called this one "The Baby", we were on our way back from a wedding fare. I was driving our biggest limo The Daddy and my wife was driving The Baby. It was a sunny afternoon; I was in front and my wife's car was several cars behind. All of a sudden a black cloud came over us and there was a massive hail storm, which swiftly covered the ground in a blanket of ice. I had lost sight of my wife and then my phone rang. It was my wife. "Come back," she said, "I have had an accident." She sounded shaken but otherwise okay, so I thought she'd had a slight bump.

Boy, was I wrong! She had gone to overtake a small van at only about 30mph on a village road, but because of the ice and the power of the car she had lost control. She went through a petrol station, narrowly missing a petrol pump, then the car had hit and wiped out a crash barrier, demolished a concrete wall, wiped out a meter square pillar, which snapped off two of the 22 inch wheels, and the car had gone airborne and come down landing on one of the, upright wheels which bent the car in two. It was a total wreck.

Fortunately, my wife seemed relatively unhurt apart from a bruised arm. But mentally I feel that incident was her breaking point and she never was the same with me again. To cut a very long story short the limo business would end five years later down the line, losing almost £200,000 that I had invested in it. It was all because of a catalog of mistakes made by the DVLA (Driver and Vehicle Licensing Authority) that resulted in my limos being rendered not fit for purpose, even though they had been inspected and a certificate had been issued by them after their inspector had personally viewed the vehicle. They had issued a V5 document, but VOSA (Vehicle Operator Standards Agency) had decided that the limo could not be used, due to it having 10 seats instead of 8 and that meant I had to take the limo off the road. The DVLA, after three years of battling, agreed that they had made a mistake and agreed that they would pay for a replacement limo at £55,000. However the manager who had made the offer to me had not got the approval, and when it was put to the Treasury for payment, they got their big-gun solicitors involved and after another couple of years they point blank refused to compensate me.

By this time my business was in tatters and so was my marriage, largely due to the pressure I had been under for almost five years of fighting the government. I even went to the House of Commons and had a meeting with my Labour MP on two separate occasions. He was convinced I was going to win. But then the government changed and I had to start the process all over again and this time I even had a meeting with the Conservative Deputy Minister of Transport in the house of commons who was convinced that mistakes had been made, but who then did a complete U-turn from saying that I had been wronged to not even returning my calls, because the DVLA had made the same mistake with another 114 limos, all of which were now deemed unfit for purpose, because of bureaucratic incompetence. And because of the sheer number the compensation would have been huge, and so they closed ranks and refused to compensate any of the owners, which destroyed my business along with countless similar small businesses around the country.

21. Rollercoaster Life

The cinema closed two years before my wife divorced me, the same year the limo business folded. Talk about a rollercoaster life. But my theory of the subatomic soul cell has continued to develop over these years. The contents of my dream, the structure of the soul, still continued to consume my thoughts. The cycle was now starting to become clear in my mind, but trying to put it into words that would enable other people to understand it was going to be my big challenge. What I found when trying to explain it, was people have been so brain washed by religion or they just don't give it any thought time at all. Ignorance is bliss, as the saying goes.

Well, as many other ground-breaking innovations which have advanced our human development over the millenniums, the basis that came from my dream had challenged me for years, although I was unraveling this exciting new possible concept to the life and death process. But whenever I tried to explain it, I could see in people's faces that they could not grasp what I was proposing. By this time I had it fairly clear in my own mind, and it presented a logical explanation which is clearly based on a cycle of the energy, and all connected to the storage of our memories in our brains. At the point of death those memories are down loaded, not to one point, but to millions of repositories where they will be used to create the future life force for subsequent generations via a subatomic bio generator. Kinetic energy is produced by using the memories which are used in a way to cause interaction in a "heaven state" to create an "emotional weight" within a million different layers that causes each layer to move independently of the other layers, forming a bio generator that produce the life force, the kinetic energy which then feeds to every single cell in the body. That small amount of energy provides the life force that sustains our being.

I know I have repeated myself. This is deliberate, to hopefully try to help you grasp this unfolding process, as what I have imparted so far is just the beginning.

22. In the Beginning

Since the beginning of the Universe energy has been present, but is there a finite amount of it, or is there a regeneration process at works that transforms energy in to different levels and forms? Could we just be part of this energy generation process, in a process that wastes nothing, and that includes our experiences emotions and our memories? So if your world is not flat come with me on a journey of "what ifs". To me it just holds incredible possibilities and is as exciting now as those who were sailing towards the horizon on that once thought flat world, and who didn't go over the edge into the abyss, but rather for them to end up in a new world of fantastic possibilities. So come with me in search of the afterlife, and learn how it is all possible. But be warned, it could confirm that Hell is a reality.

Life on this planet is one of our first contradictions in the reasoning process between religion and logic, and that was that the Earth was created in six days, or was it in sixty billion years? Was it created by God or natural forces, or are they one and the same? How are we to believe what our elders wrote in the Bible, one of the books which is so highly regarded by establishments that still in the 21st Century preach is as the "Gospel" And yet so many of the stories within its covers have been proven incorrect or fanciful embellishments of hearsay over the ages. And yet this is the foundation of some of the most powerful and wealthy "organizations" in the world, whose existence, if analyzed, would be condemned by their own rules. And these so-called "Houses of God" instigate wars and corruption throughout this world and are thus guilty of so much that is wrong. I know I said I would not preach or condemn anyone's religion. So OK, I lied. But isn't that the way of this world. I apologize not for what I have said about religion, and that includes all religions, but for the fact I said I wouldn't condemn them. If I am going to get you to

212

accept my theory you MUST first do away with religion as it truly does not have a part in the logic of "heaven". The myths that have been preached over the millennium has corrupted the truth of the life and death process which has to be biological, not mythical. There must be a biological process and what I have began to explain to you must, I feel, come closer to the truth than the airy fairy stories of a factually incorrect book.

The accepted processes of creation to a religious person, is that the Almighty did it in six days, and then on the seventh day he rested. This, to me, is a real flat world moment. Yes I should respect the right of people to accept this explanation, but it is wrong. It was not created in six days!

There is a somewhat more plausible scientific explanation, of course, and this I feel happier with. So for the purpose of my theory, we will take it that the World wasn't created in six days. But now where did life come from? Again we have conflict here; religion tells us Adam created Eve by taking one of his own ribs, and then after a lot more begetting we now have nearly seven billion people on the planet. Sorry, but I again tend to go for the science and Darwin's theory of evolution, yet this still does not explain or even give the whole picture of the life and death process. This planet is constantly changing, and in order to survive we have had to adapt and evolve, and to date there has not been a clear explanation as to how we have managed to do it. Genetics has provided the basis of how our physiological form has adapted to our environment. But what of our minds and the increase of intelligence of our species, how has this progressed and improved over time? And why and how do we have child prodigies? Science has not explained this adequately to my mind. So let's look at it from the "Logical Beginning"

When the Earth was formed it was first a collection of rocks that spun in the heavens and over a very long time. It doesn't matter how long it was; just that it wasn't six days, and it eventually formed into two bodies - the Earth and the Moon. It was in fact formed from hundreds of trillions of bodies throughout the universe, but for our purpose we will concentrate on our own micro-environment, the Earth and its moon. When the Earth cooled and water formed on the surface from the collisions with tens of thousands of icy comets, the water from those comets contained, we are told, "the building blocks of life". I believe they also contained a wonderful component: the "life force" (or if you prefer, the souls) which were also present in the water, as water is the most basic requirement to sustain life Why should it not then also be the repository, essence of, and origination of its life force. Surely it stands to reason that is so.

The properties of water are many and the most important, I feel sure, are yet to be discovered, but which form the basis of many of the answers which I have conceived, and that it has now formed the foundation of the subatomic soul cell theory. I hope as you are reading through this book, that you will change many of your own views on this existence we call life.

Second Peter 35 - 8:

For this concealed from them intentionally that the heaven and earth of old were in the water having been exhibited by the word of God.

As I mentioned earlier I feel this passage in the Bible could hold the answer to the secret of the location of the soul, heaven, and or life force. But as I also said earlier I don't hold store with a lot of what the Bible has promoted, as the level of mistakes which exist within its pages, if you spend the time to question it, leaves the reader confused. And the most incredulous to my mind, apart from Noah and the Great Flood, is that Christ was born of a virgin. I believe this story came about as the result of a mistake in the translation from Hebrew to Greek, because the original script said that Christ was born of a young woman, and so we had one of the classic mistakes which embellished the sensational story that the King of the Jews was born of a virgin.

Notwithstanding my criticisms, however, I do believe that there is a great deal of information within the Bible that offers a great deal of wisdom. Peter 35-8, for example, completely established that the souls are in the water. For many people the word "soul" conjures up a religious element, but it is just a name for a tangible component. Just like a heart or brain, the soul is a component of the whole. It is the origin of the life force or the God particle, the centre of us being an entity. In the soul I feel that we are dealing

217

with a multi-functional device and the "reason" why we are here!

23. Origin of the Soul

Throughout the ages the soul has been written about by almost every philosopher; all have their own interpretation of its purpose, some romantic some more practical but all have their own theories of what the soul is. The origin of the soul has been a controversial question in Christian history. Two points of view may be distinguished: creationism, which posits that God creates each individual soul in a special act of creation (at the time of conception according to some or that of birth according to others), and traducianism, which suggests that the parents in begetting the child beget the soul too. The creationist principle has generally held sway in Christianity.

Aristotle defined the soul as the first actuality of a natural organized body but argued against it having a separate existence from the physical body. In Aristotle's view, the primary activity of a living thing constitutes its soul; for example, the soul of an eye, if it were an independent organism, would be seeing (its purpose or final cause).The various faculties of the soul or psyche, such as nutrition, sensation, movement, and so forth, when exercised, constitute the "second" actuality, or fulfillment, of the capacity to be alive. A good example is someone who falls asleep, as opposed to someone who falls dead; the former actuality can wake up and go about their life, while the second actuality can no longer do so. Plato, drawing on the words of his teacher Socrates, considered the soul the essence of a person, being that which decides how we behave. He considered this essence to be an incorporeal, eternal occupant of our being. As bodies die, the soul is continually reborn in subsequent bodies. The Platonic soul comprises three parts:

1) the Logos (mind, nous or reason)

2) the Thymo or thumetikon (emotion or spiritedness, or masculine)

3) the Eros or epithumetikon (appetitive, or desire, or feminine)

Each of these has a function in a balanced, level and peaceful soul. Aristotle identified three hierarchical levels of living things: plants, animals, and people, for which groups he identified three corresponding levels of soul, or biological activity: the nutritive activity of growth, sustenance and reproduction which all life shares; the self-willed motive activity and sensory faculties, which only animals and people have in common; and finally reason, of which people alone are capable. The ancient Greeks used the same word for 'alive' as for 'ensouled', indicating that the earliest surviving western philosophical view believed that the soul was that which gave the body life. The soul was considered the incorporeal or spiritual 'breath' which animates Erwin Rohde writes

221

that the early pre-Pythagorean belief was that the soul had no life when it departed from the body, and retired into Hades or Hell with no hope of returning to a body. It has been argued that a strict line of causality fails to explain certain phenomena within human experience (such as free will) that have at times been attributed to the soul. Some metaphysical thinkers believe that the concept of soul can be a solution for the explanatory gap and the problem of other minds which suggests that we cannot know if other people really have consciousness (Socrates and Plato).

Christian religions have a variety of beliefs relating to the soul. It is my belief that the soul is the combination of the spirit and body. The spirit and the body is the soul of man. In Genesis 2:7 we read, *"And the LORD God formed man [of] the dust of the ground, and breathed into his nostrils the breath of life; and man became a living soul."*

'The breath of life' in this case is the spirit of man which is the life the body (James 2:26), and God is literally the Father of our spirits (Hebrews 12:9). I should point out from the above Geneses verse, verse seven, that everyone born into the world is formed from the dust of the ground, and to the dust of the ground we shall return. In the first resurrection of the righteous and in the second resurrection of the wicked, body and spirit shall be inseparably joined and shall live for ever.

Most doctors won't even get into any meaningful conversation about the soul and its location. It is almost as if they possibly know more than they are letting on, but are forbidden to divulge its secrets. I have always found it strange and almost worrying, that doctors who repair our bodies daily and perform autopsies, still don't know where the soul resides, or if it has weight. In 1901 Dr Duncan MacDougall made weight measurements of patients as they died. He claimed that there was weight loss of varying amounts at the time of death. His results have never been successfully reproduced, and are therefore scientifically meaningless.

Clearly even in religious terms there must be some kind of connection between the soul and our life force, that is our "spiritual" existence. Without it there is just an empty shell. The body is therefore seen as the vessel that contains our god given existence, that we can use during our time of "life" but it is almost treated as two separate items: our conscience and soul which are two different entities, as if one is at a state of the "keeper" of our soul, and then the soul itself which is something that can either reap the rewards of our "good" existence on Earth, or if we do not lead a good life our soul will suffer in damnation of hell for eternity.

So it's as if religion see it as three separate things the "Body or Vessel", the "Keeper or Who we are", and the "Soul" the gift, which we must look after.

Although, at the point of death nothing appears to leave the body, well not in the visual sense of the word, again this point is highly written about. Religion would have us believe, that our soul rises up to Heaven or down into the fiery pit of Hell, but again, with all the advancements of space travel and powerful telescopes, that have looked deep into space and yet, Heaven has not been located "up there ". As for Hell, down there, well I think probably not, so as for anything leaving the body at death on a spiritual basis is pretty much, I feel, unlikely. Although I think a lot of people if asked would have the images as portrayed by the movie industry in films like "Ghost" where our Soul or Spirit is taken to another place by angels or demon's "the spiritual form" that is would be more acceptable to them. But these are ideas which have focused on the religious fears and threats of control employed by the Churches over the centuries to control the congregations! But none offer a useful solution where there is a true purpose to our existence and our passing.

FACT: Death occurs when the life force stops!

24. The Given Soul

At what point are we given our soul? Where does it come from? One would expect it to be at the point of conception, but there is no evidence that this is the case. However, as this is the fundamental point in our creation why are we not researching and looking for something so important to our existence. We frequently see on the Discovery Channel the incredible footage of the point where the sperm penetrates the egg and bang we have the creation of a new being. But where is this life force, the soul? We can clearly see the sperm enter the egg and then the cell starts splitting and dividing over and over again, but still no soul or life force "is visible", or is there? It makes you wonder! Just let us suppose for one minute that at the point of conception as the sperm penetrates the egg, that at the very point of contact there is a particle of energy which is so incredibly small that it has not as yet been detected by human technology. This particle, I believe, is caught between the sperm and the egg, thus all three components are then in evolved in the fusion of life, the creation reaction, that this particle triggers is so small that as yet it has been undetected by human technology and yet it is there. And that this particle contains within it, not only the trigger of the process, but it provides the "life-force" or if you want to call it the Soul or Spirit. So now, and it only hypothetical, we have the "battery" that will power and not only start the creation process, but it will sustain that life until it one day is extinguished by whatever means that causes that being to cease to be. Remember that this whole process takes place in fluid (made up of water) so surely it not impossible that there is something else within that fluid. Anyway, I ask you, for the sake of my theory, to go along with me and accept that there is a third component to the conception of a new life, and that it does supply the "life force" to the fusion of the egg and the sperm to create a new person.

Back to my dream: After I finished traveling up the tube-like pipe lines, which I reasoned was the nervous system, I ended up at the empty memory cells of the host which were black and completely finished with, which brought me to a point of complete frustration because this was what I had expected was the case. The thought that it was all a waste, even though I had witnessed the workings of the Soul Cell, the one question was still unanswered - why? Then it was as if I passed out, as everything went black, and when I came to I was in a completely new and equally alien environment. But the feeling of bereavement and sadness had changed. Now there was warmth and a feeling of joy, and the sound of the pounding which had been with me the whole time until the death of the individual was now back, but much faster and somehow very different, inducing a feeling of jubilation. Then I could make out I was in a watery fluid, but it was as if it was populated by millions of transparent jellyfish. I was completely surrounded in

229

what I now recognized as Soul Cells, millions upon millions of them, and every single one looked totally different from the next one, almost as if each one had its own individual personality. It was like walking down a busy street and looking at the faces of people walking past you; they all look so totally different, well that's how it seemed.

Then my guide's instruction came - "*Watch and witness the miracle of creation*" - and with that, it was as if a school of sharks appeared from out of the distance, but it was a race and they were jostling for position. Then I could see another planet in the distance, but it looked almost hairy or spiky. I then realized what was going on, and where I was; this was conception and the sharks were sperm, and the hairy planet was the egg. Then, as if in slow motion, I saw one of the sperm attacking the egg, almost in the fashion of a kamikaze pilot. Everything to me looked massive; the egg was, as I said, a planet floating in this sea of souls. In comparison, a single soul cell was the equivalent to a tiny tennis ball, and the sperm were like massive jumbo jets. But as everything was happening in slow motion, I witnessed the most incredible thing of my life. As one of the jumbo jets impacted into the planet, just one of the tennis balls was at the very tip of the point of penetration, out of the billions of them just one soul cell had been caught in that point and was instantly injected into the egg as the jumbo passed through the surface. At that point I felt a shock wave as the planet's skin erupted and changed from a soft penetrable object, to what now was solid and all the other jumbo jets just bounced off its surface. Still in slow motion, at that same instant there was a fantastic reaction within the planet. There was a very bright explosion and the surface of the soul cell was ripped off and all the barcodes were sent spinning around the inside of the egg, and the sperm also exploded, so it became like a clear soup of the components of the sperm and the soul cell surface, which for a while looked like it was in a washing machine. There was what I can only describe as lightning or sparks coming out from the surface of the tiny soul cell as it span in the center of the egg and slowly the soup cleared and slowed down and all the barcodes and the soul cell started to vibrate fiercely, then every single item was duplicated including the soul cell and they moved to opposite sides, so there were two whirlpools spinning in opposite directions each side of the egg.

Then the egg started having what looked like contractions and began to form into an infinity symbol, and then twisted and locked off, the two sections each, with its own soul cell and a complete set of barcodes. Then I could see that the soul cells were giving off the lightning again, and so the cells divided, again and again.

and every time the new soul cells were the catalyst to the cell division, then the process picked up speed, and it was like watching that movie on the Discovery channel again, and within a very short time I was looking at a human fetus in the very early stages But as each cell divided there was a complete copy of the soul cell within each and every cell of that baby, and that soul cell was like a little battery which was not only responsible for the kick start to that cell and life, but it would continue to power every single cell within that person, until one day they would once again receive the download that would finalize the process once again. Whether the barcodes were the DNA or a prelude to the DNA cell creation, I don't know, but the process was a miracle. In fact I'm pretty sure it was not the DNA as they were far too small. I came to the conclusion that they were the intelligence and the instructions that controlled the whole process, including the DNA.

25. Intelligence Injection

I hope you can agree with me that there must be that third component to the conception process, and that it is the life-force/Soul/Spirit, or whatever you want to call it! It stands to reason that it must be present as the sperm and the egg come together and as it is not clearly visible it must be at this present time undetectable to us. But the one thing I am convinced about is that my theory of the Subatomic Soul Cell could be the logical explanation to this process. As far as I know there is no other plausible or otherwise tangible explanation out there to explain this part of the start of the life process.

Now I would ask you to bear with me for this next part. As I said earlier, we understand that the genetics can account for the physiological development of the species, but what about the intelligence, and how we adapt to our habitat. There must be a process where this information is passed on down the line.

Remember those rain forest monkeys that just know not to eat the poison berries that will kill them. Or birds that can navigate the planet without instruction. I totally believe that there is a mechanism that works hand-in-hand with the creation and life force process that at the point of conception imparts additional information to that new being, that is in addition to that what the male and female parents impart. I feel sure this is why we have children who demonstrate characteristics that neither parent possesses, and I believe this is how we get the child prodigies who are able to play the piano or have other talents in mathematics and the like, without having had a single lesson and without either of the parents being able to play an instrument or have a high level of intelligence. I'm sure you will agree that there must be some explanation as to why we have these anomalies in intelligence and abilities.

So we have the life force and now we possibly have intelligence being introduced to the creation of a new being. How does this happen and where do these particles come from? And how do they have this ability to impart information which could be responsible for the kick starting of the life process? So once again I return to my dream. This time let's look at the skin between each layer or each entity "heaven zone". You remember I told you that it looked like the skin had been scorched and that something had been removed from it. Well it is my understanding of the dream that at the point of death, after the download of memories and emotions is complete, the final process is to form the skin around the soul cell which finalizes life of the being. But at the very end the last thing to happen is all of the abilities and intelligence of that individual are also downloaded from the brain and are put on to the skin, imprinted into what looked to me as if they were bar codes, although, which were far more organic, and squiggly, than the actual bar codes that you would see on a can of baked beans in a supermarket. The entire surface of the soul cell was covered in what seem to be hundreds of wavy organic bar codes. This I felt in the dream is crucial information to the continuation life process as explained and stripped off in the conception process. The violent reaction that begins the life process in the conception of a new human, which is the fusion of the main components that delivers the package of "DNA " from the mother and the father. But also there is the life force which has never been detected in either the sperm or the egg, which for my theory is delivered via the subatomic soul cell. This provides not only the energy within that soul cell to fire the creation reaction but even provides the instructions that through the process of fusion of the components, the surface of that soul cell is stripped down, thereby releasing all of the bar codes which contain a vast quantity of information, including instructions for the construction of the

237

baby, the intelligence and the adaption to habitat information, which are all impregnated into the cell of the developing fetus. The cell division process now underway within each individual cell is a complete copy of the set of the DNA which is established now. But fifty years ago, if someone was told that there was this code in your body that contains the blueprint of your body's construction, they would have said "You're bloody mad" and yet not so long after it was first discovered DNA is now a buzz word; we all know how big a part it plays in our lives. But the DNA is what I will call the "components of construction", whereas the SSC (Subatomic Soul Cell) is the Architect or Controller that tells each individual strand of DNA to connect to which other strand of DNA to either construct, say a leg of a certain length or a hand of certain size or an eye of a certain color. It is the SSC that, like the DNA code book, is duplicated in every new cell. But the SSC is the brain of that cell giving the instructions to the

DNA strands because I believe each DNA strand contains one or more SSC at its core. During the construction of the brain the SSC continue to impart the basic intelligence to enable the fetus to continue through the development process.

Sometimes a SSC may have had as its last host someone who had a particular talent, and when the basic and more stronger information is imparted to the fetus there is an additional download of specific information which was part of the download at the point that the previous host had died. If it was one of the SSC of, say, "Mr Mozart" for example, then the lucky recipient may inherit qualities that neither the mother or the father possessed. This, perhaps, does not only apply to a talent; it could be an educational quality, or even facial beauty. How many times have you looked at someone's child and thought, well, they didn't get it from their parents. It's all because of the third component: the SSC.

239

Just to repeat the process again, let's say Mr Mozart is just about to die. His body goes into stage one; his body and his SSCs go into a state of readiness. The adrenalin shock kicks in, which I have felt several times, and opens up the nervous system, down to the umbilical cord which until now has been a one way system delivering the life force from SSC. But now it has to be made ready to carry a colossal amount of information. Next, his memories start to flash before what he thinks are his eyes. He then experiences going down a long tunnel (the nervous system and then the umbilical) cord to the SSCs. He enters what he now believes is Heaven, ever moving towards the light (the light of the nucleus of the atom) and his memories which had arrived at the SSCs before what is left of his conscience, senses people who he remembers and he believes that they are welcoming him to Heaven. Now if Mozart was going to be an NDE survivor his conscience would from this place return back up the umbilical cord to his brain, and he

240

could then be revived, and describe all his wonderful experiences, as Dr Eden Alexander in the "*Proof of Heaven*" was able to do. However, sadly for Mr Mozart his time had come to its end, and the final state is achieved, which is the finalization of his SSCs. Because every single cell in Mozart's body contains one of his SSC and every one of them had received a copy of the download from Mr Mozart's brain.

Finalization now starts, which means first, a skin is formed around the entire SSC, then the umbilical cord starts to detach, but before it breaks away it acts like a laser which is ready to etch into the entire skin surface what comes from an additional download of information. This is fed down to the tip of the umbilical cord and is then imprinted on to the skin in the form of what I said looked like a biological barcode that contains most importantly the instructions that triggers the next conception process, if and when this SSC is fortunate to be at that precise point, between the egg and the sperm. The skin's barcode will also contain instructions for the DNA to enable the fetus to develop and grow. Then there will be adoption to habitat information like (don't eat the berries; they will kill you), followed by the basic "computer code" which will be located in the brain that will control the vital functions such as breathing, etc.. And finally there may be some of Mr Mozart's unique abilities imprinted onto the skin. At which point the life force generator of Mr Mozart turns off and he is dead.

Now things get interesting in Mr Mozart's body. His conscience has gone but every cell in his body is a little ball of energy. And it wants to find a new host; that is its mission. Meanwhile Mr Mozart's memories are now being used. Is his conscience aware that he has died? I have two trains of thought for this which I will come back to later

Do you remember that umbilical cord that so precisely engraved the skin of the SSC that is now a weapon of war and the remains of poor old Mr Mozart is its enemy and its mission is to systematically destroy every one of Mr Mozart's cells and then the umbilical laser. Then one by one turns all the cells turn to mush. We know this as putrefaction. These SSCs want to be released. So these SSCs are then eventually released via cremation or interment, via putrefaction, back, into the environment within the molecules of water and water vapor which we constantly breathe in, drink and which makes up such a large percentage of our entire body. And surprise surprise, it is even in the fluid that the sperm and egg are suspended in, and then by accidental and totally random selection, just one of the subatomic soul cells will be the catalyst of the creation of a brand new life.

Right, so it contains the life force, so therefore it has fulfilled the function of the soul or spirit. It's a multi functional cell and it is the very essence of life and death, because when it stops death is pronounced.

How does it work? Reincarnation is an interesting theory, believed by many to be the answer to our existence as a new entity, whether a butterfly or a human they all have "the essence of life", the "life force", and why shouldn't it be the same life force? They all begin with the same cell division process, so could there be an element of creation which is common to all life forms? If the answer is yes, it begs the question does the butterfly have a soul? If in the reincarnation process we share souls with other species how would that work? I can't answer this but my theory may go some way to addressing the issue later. However, reincarnation may well be closer to the answer than we realize, because one of the laws of the Universe is that nothing is totally destroyed, it merely changes its state. You can burn something which appears to be destroyed, but its properties still exists in an atomic level as gases, and carbon, so let's apply this to our soul/life force. We die, but whether we are cremated or interred, over time our chemical state changes. And the components are released back into their basic elements, and eventually blow in the wind. Ashes to ashes, dust to dust, water to water vapor. Let's assume what happens to our body, also happens to our soul. The soul must also be released into the environment, so why not assume they are reused in the re-creation process or reincarnation; not a reincarnation of the person but of the soul is reincarnated to a new host.

My mother was a strong believer in reincarnation. I suppose this encouraged my thinking in this direction, although I believe my mother thought that it was possible to come back as a flower or a bird. But if we have no conscience of that transition then it is not effectively us who comes back. But my mother was right in the chemical sense. Yes, some of our chemicals will undoubtedly be used in other living things eventually. But that's not quite what I have in mind, although in real terms our chemicals are dispersed and once in the environment they can and will be recycled into many shapes and forms.

But what of the "entity", the conscience of that person "us" - that thing that makes us who we are? Why shouldn't it also be recycled? This is one of my strongest beliefs that because nothing is wasted everything has a purpose and everything is for a purpose. So what is this purpose of the soul? Remember, energy, power, life force, the construction of the subatomic soul cell. I believe that the soul is this incredible bio or physical/static/kinetic life force energy generator. You should by now be seeing the possibilities of my theory.

26. Types of Souls

For my theory to work there would have to be two separate subatomic soul cells that exist in two different states. And as I have explained, there would have to be both types of soul cell - active and passive - for the theory to work. The "Passive to Active" soul cells being the ones which start the life cycle at conception of a new being and are then duplicated via the cell splitting process as each cell is created and becoming the Active Soul Cell. Then connected to a soul cell system in any living being, providing the life force required for that being to sustain life. "Passive to Active" soul cells are those which have been finalized and are freely distributed in the environment; floating soul cells that are constantly around us, just as pollen is. They are totally invisible because of the size and construction of the subatomic soul cell. So you see, we are existing in a sea of souls, which we ingest constantly without out even realizing it. However, both types of soul cell give us energy, but only the Active soul is connected to the life force process, as it is fixed within every single cell of our body and being at the very centre of every cell in our body, they remain there until the death process once again releases them, and that happens when they are once again finalized and locked until they one day are again involved in another conception process. The Passive soul cells pass through our body during breathing, drinking and eating, and as they do they impart to us small amounts of energy as part of our body energy consumption and regeneration and the revitalization processes.

It has occurred to me that there may be a two part generation process going on between the Passive and the Active soul cells within the body, although I am not entirely sure of this at the moment. But I continue to ponder this, as deep down I think that the interaction between these two types (of what are effectively negative and positive soul cells) could be a big part of the life force energy process that sustains us.

27. Human Intelligence

For thousands of years in man's evolution and technological development of civilizations there were things which happened that are extremely puzzling. For example, I have always been intrigued and deeply interested in the Egyptian's Egyptology. I supposed it was their passion for the afterlife and in particularly the development of the Pyramids, having shaped structures that seem to have happened around the globe at a similar time, when there has been no tangible likelihood of any travel between vastly different civilizations. I am referring to the Incas in Peru, the Mayans in Mexico and the Aztecs in south America, not forgetting the Chinese in China and of course the Egyptians in Egypt, who are distributed all around the world and yet at roughly the same time, without any form of known communication between these different civilizations, they all came up with the same shaped structure - the "Pyramid" - completely independently of each other to form the tombs for their afterlife. Yes it could be a coincidence once or twice, but this was repeated time and time again over the four corners of the globe. How?

Well, the Subatomic Soul Cell Theory can easily explain what has happened and it is the very same reason that we have gifted child protégés, another mystery that has basically remained unanswered until now. The answer lies in what happens at the point of death. As I have mentioned earlier the download process from the brain to the Soul cells happens in a split-second. Every experience and emotion that you have ever had is imparted to that soul cell and the final thing that happens which finalizes the death process is the formation of the skin or shell around the soul. But as that skin is formed a final download of intelligence and artistic abilities is imprinted on the skin in such a way that allows them to be ingested into the creation process. It is my belief that the skin or shell of the soul cell is multi-functional. As I said, it concludes the life of the host being and forms the barrier that will separate that entity forevermore. But I am sure it also contains valuable downloaded information other than memories and emotions. I think it contains evolutionary information such as adaption to habitat, and educational and artistic abilities which are also downloaded at the point of the death of the host, because all this information is imprinted into the surface of the skin or shell of that soul cell and will remain there, but over time will start to fade and becomes weaker.

Returning now to the question of child protégés, you will remember that I explained that at the point of conception we have three elements to consider, namely the sperm from the father, the egg from the mother, and you have the subatomic soul cell which gives the life force, and all three create that new being who becomes the host in the subatomic soul cell system. But just say that neither the mother nor the father could play the piano and yet at the age of three that new being without any piano lessons is able to play that piano like Bach. So how is this possible?

Let us suppose that the subatomic soul cell that was imparted at the point of conception was from a previous host who, say, had conceived the pyramid, and that soul cell did more than just impart the life force; it also uploaded some of his abilities as an accomplished pyramid builder, and that's how I explain the existence of the similar structures around the world. Similarly, a gifted child's astounding ability can be explained in this way.

Don't feel hard done by if you are not an accomplished pianist or a mastermind like Albert Einstein. After all, you did get your ability to continue to adapt to your environment, just like the monkeys in the rainforest who if they eat a certain wild berry will die, so along the line, one of the monkeys who ate the berry died and that information was imprinted onto his subatomic soul cell, thus the next generation of monkey who received one of the dead monkey's subatomic soul cells is imparted with "don't eat those berries" and eventually all monkeys are created with the "don't eat the berries that will kill you" cell. But are these Subatomic Soul Cells transferable from one species to another? I don't think so. I think each species has its own Subatomic Soul Cell group which is dictated by nature. You don't have cats breading with dogs, so why should their subatomic soul cells be any different? But, yes, as with the monkey, all animals (and even plants) have subatomic "soul" cells. It is part of the life energy cycle of all living things.

You have to try to let go of thousands of years of religious indoctrination that the "soul" is just a spiritual thing. So going back to my example of the Pyramid builders, how do several completely separated civilizations with no record of any direct contact at roughly the same time come up with the same idea? You will recall that I said the subatomic soul cells of grains of pollen are floating all around us, just blowing in the wind, and flowing in the sea: that's how the subatomic soul cells are distributed around the planet. And that's how the idea of the pyramid was conceived by several different civilizations at roughly the same time, although it would have been over tens of generations. The subatomic soul cells carry the information between the continents. As the idea was conceived by one individual who died, his subatomic soul cells were released and traveled around the world in the winds. They were then ingested into the conception process on several different continents and as those human beings continued to develop their minds, with each new generation the concept of the pyramid also developed, and that's why they are slightly different in appearances, but nevertheless a basic pyramid shape. That's how my theory explains how civilizations who never ever physically came into contact with one another, still managed to come up with the same basic idea.

So I can hear you ask, why are we all not geniuses or Sebastian Bach's? Well for one thing, "Mother Nature" loves the numbers game. There are far more ordinary people on the planet than geniuses, so it stands to reason you are more likely to get a bog standard or ordinary basic run of the mill subatomic soul cell than one from a genius. But also, as with all things in nature, over time the outer skin or shell starts to decay or deplete or for the want of a better word it fades. So when the subatomic soul cell is involved in the conception process it does its main job of imparting a life force, but when it comes to intelligence information less is available to be ingested by that new being and so, like me, you are an average being. This degrading process also has the effect of ensuring that we don't get an ancient soul cell that would be a backward step. No, Mother Nature wants us to develop and improve our intelligence. However, if you are lucky to get a nice fresh subatomic soul cell that hasn't been through the mill, don't forget the Passive subatomic soul cell has a secondary purpose in that, until it is ingested into the conception process, it is passing through bodies providing secondary energy.

Secondary energy? Yes, because once the Passive subatomic soul is ingested into the conception process it becomes an "Active" Subatomic Soul Cell, but those subatomic soul cells that are waiting for their opportunity to become Active, remain Passive bio energy generators, which we get when we eat drink and even breathe. The Passive subatomic soul cells just pass through and energize us which all contributes to our internal life force. You may that that it is food that gives us our energy, but that is a calorie based energy that feeds our muscles and is a totally different type of energy from the life force energy. Let me put it like this. Coal has energy locked up within it; we can burn it and get heat energy, but if we use the heat from the coal burning to boil water that drives an electrical generator then we have a totally different energy - electrical energy - but neither the coal energy or the electrical energy is life force energy. There are many different types of energy.

I just wanted to demonstrate in my logical way that there are many types of energy, and so it is with the life force. So please don't confuse life force energy with the energy we get from food, coal or electricity. Subatomic soul cell energy is the essence of life that powers our being. It's an energy that is so pure, yet so small, which is delivered so deep within our being that it has remained undetectable to human examination. Yet it's a fact that every day we have existed on it without question. There is no doubt it is there sustaining us, so what further proof could you ask for? It is something that I needed to understand and share. Life exists, therefore there must be a logical explanation for it, and that's all I have tried to provide, by applying my theory to it. It offers something that could be the answer

28. Home of the Soul

This is what you have all been waiting for, and the answer is a mystery not as to it location but the fact that this has not been realized or considered before now, because with all the conclusions that I have made throughout this book, you should by now be coming to the same conclusion that I have regarding the location of the soul, or as my theory requires: "Souls".

But before I totally give the game away I will give you some scientific facts which helped me to confirm my reasoning about this part of my theory. If the soul is going to be in the body, which it really must be, then it stands to reason that it would be connected to the majority of the major parts of the body or at least to the brain. However, are we still thinking of the soul as a religious phenomenon or a logical viable component of the overall function of the human body? If at this point you are still considering the

260

"religious soul" then you really have completely missed the message in this book, but I wouldn't blame you because of the "brain washing" that goes on from kindergarten, and because of your conditioning you feel that any other explanation about the soul would be wrong. If, however, you are looking for evidence as to the validity of my theory, I ask you first to consider how much evidence is there to the alleged "religious soul" and I am sure you will find that my theory has far more going for it than the thousands of years of religious mumbo jumbo and mental conditioning that you have been subjected to that tells you absolutely nothing tangible at all. Religious preaching expects you to believe everything unconditionally. I fully accept that my theory may have large holes in it and it will probably be ridiculed by many. But to my mind there are precious few good explanations out there, so next, in my penultimate chapter, are twenty crucial questions that must be answered to support the credibility of my theory.

29. The Answers

Where did we come from?

Answer: It is pretty much agreed that life on this planet started with the arrival of water, via comets, and this fits with my theory. That life and indeed our life force was suspended in that element, but not just as the building blocks of life, but in the form of Subatomic Soul Cells. I believe that these subatomic soul cells were the mechanism that enabled the evolution process to begin and continue to where we are today. So there are two facets in this first question. The first is that it is in the water as a components of the H_2O atomic structure, and secondly that the subatomic soul cell is the device which has enabled us to progress our intelligence over the millenniums.

Water (H_2O) is often perceived to be ordinary as it is transparent, odorless, tasteless and ubiquitous. It is the simplest compound of the two most common reactive elements, consisting of just two hydrogen atoms attached to a single oxygen atom. Indeed, very few molecules are smaller or lighter. Liquid water, however, is the most extraordinary substance. Although we drink it, wash, fish and swim in it, and cook with it (although probably not all at the same time), we nearly always overlook the special relationship it has with our lives. Droughts cause famines and floods cause death and disease. It makes up over about half of us and, without it we die within a few days. Water has importance as a solvent, a solute, a reactant and a biomolecule, structuring proteins, nucleic acids and cells and controlling our consciousness. H_2O is the second most common molecule in the Universe (behind hydrogen, H_2), the most abundant solid material and fundamental to star formation. There is a hundred times as many water molecules in our bodies as the sum of all the other molecules put together. Life cannot evolve or continue without liquid water, which is why there is so much excitement about finding it on Mars and other planets and moons. It is unsurprising that water plays a central role in many of the World's religions.

Water properties

Water is the most studied material on Earth but it is remarkable to find that the science behind its behavior and function are so poorly understood (or even ignored), not only by people in general, but also by scientists working with it every day. It can be extremely slippery and extremely sticky at the same time. The small size of its molecule belies the complexity of its actions and its singular capabilities. Liquid water's unique properties and chameleonic nature seem to fit ideally into the requirements for life as can no other molecule. A number of explanations of the complex behavior of liquid water have been published, many quite recently, with several stirring up great controversy. So I am confident that water will one day give up the answers that will prove my theory to be correct.

Is there a reincarnation process?

Answer: My theory describes a multi-generation particle that is used over and over again. New life does not start until a Subatomic Soul Cell is at the point of the conception the creation process for that new entity. It is the soul which is reincarnated, although the transfer of information is not of an individual nature - so no, we do not get reincarnated. Our entire existence is part of the continuing life process. But looking at this same question from a another viewpoint, the answer is yes and no. No, we as individuals do not become reincarnated after our existence has come to an end, as we have served our purpose. But yes, our soul will go on after we die as it did before we became a live being, and when our time is up our soul will continue to be reused time and time again.

If you have not yet realized it, according to my theory there is a purpose to life that fits into the order of things. The souls is a life force generator and the reason we are here is to provide the energy in the form of our memories and emotions to constantly refuel the soul cell of future generations, and it is the potential difference in the emotions of each layer of the soul cell that cause the layers to revolve, due to their emotional weight; as the layers spin there is either a static or kinetic process that give to soul cell an output charge, which emanates out from the soul poles into the matter around the cell. If they are Active soul cells they directly inject the power into our body, whereas if they are Passive soul cells they emit energy into the environment they are suspended in, which is of course water and water vapor, the source and sustainer of all life.

The energy from the passive soul cell can be clearly seen in the human aura and the colour of the Aura depends on the dominant emotion being omitted from the hundreds of trillions of soul cells which are attracted to that individual. I totally agree this is a radical theory, yet so many of its facets in principle work and as there are no other explanations to most of these questions, let alone all of them, and the fact that each individual component of my theory fits with the others, and when you put it together with the information in Dr Alexander's book "*The Proof of Heaven*", I feel deeply that we are looking at "*The Logic of Heaven*".

Where is the Soul?

Answer: My theory is based on a great deal of scientific reasoning, and I cannot believe that it has not been considered by far more intelligent people than myself, because the solution has been staring everyone in the face. Why should we just have one Soul? Yes we start with one Soul, the random selection of a soul that is at the reaction point between the sperm and the egg, the creation point of our very own Big Bang, that miraculous moment in time when a new life starts. It could be any one of a billion souls that are present at the creation area. Then there is the transfer of the kick-start and the freshness and condition of that particular soul and of the previous occupant will determine what information is contributed to the new being. The human body consists of over 60% water, which has the atomic structure of "H_2O". Throughout this book I have explained that for the subatomic soul cell to work, you have to have a "potential difference" for energy to flow. My theory defines two types of subatomic soul cell: Passive and Active. If out of curiosity we suppose that the "O" of the H_2O, the oxygen atom, is the location of the Active Subatomic Soul Cell and the hydrogen atoms (H_2) are the location of the Passive Subatomic Soul Cells, the Hydrogen are at a charge of minus 28 and oxygen atoms are at charge of plus 8, we have the potential difference that is needed for my theory to function. So the answer to where are the souls seems clear to me; I believe they are in the water, and why shouldn't they be, when you consider that life on this planet came from water? That all may have sounded plausible or not, but the honest answer is I don't know where the soul or souls are. But one thing is for sure, they are out of the range of today's science so I am sure they are invisible, probably because they are pure energy - there is little or no actual substance to them - although I'm sure they are in there somewhere in the water as water is full of energy. Life force requires energy and this has to be generated. At the point of death emotions and memories are energy signals, so many people who have had a NDE have explained that their lives flashed before their eyes and at the end of the tunnel they could see their loved ones. If we accept my download theory as the possible regeneration process and the energy that is emitted from the subatomic soul cells is the provider of the life force, and the surplus subatomic souls cells are responsible for the human aura, and the reason that clairvoyants are able to read "messages" from the departed and even the subconscious receiving some of the omissions from subatomic soul cell that are passing that part of the brain that is responsible for dreams, hence, we have varied dreams which are made up partly of our own memories and partly of those encapsulated in that subatomic soul cell passing through the brain's blood cells which is rich with passive subatomic soul cells.

What is the Soul?

Answer: The "Soul" almost dominated my dream and started to consolidate everything that I had considered over the years in my search for answers. The thing that came out of the dream was that the soul is a multi functional "Cell" (an Orb) which has several properties. Its main property is similar to the hard drive or memory storage device in a computer, the ROM (read only memory), set out in concentric, decreasing rings, each ring separated by a skin or shell, of the multi-layered cell. Each layer is the essence of a previous being, building up like rings on a tree. The skin is also like computer memory but this time RAM (read and write memory) which is required to form part of the life force generation, the main function of the Soul Cell. At the point of death the entire memory banks of the brain are downloaded between the last layer and the top layer skin of the cell. At the point of death the cell is "finalized" similarly to the process of writing a DVD which when finalized concludes the DVD and in the soul

271

concludes the life of "that" being. As soon as the finalization is complete the body starts to putrefy, thereby releasing the soul cells to the environment. To visualize the soul cell, imagine it as if it is like the planet Earth, with the crust, the magma, and the core. In my dream I could clearly see the orb in cross section. The skin was clearly visible in the cross section and the skin of the cell contained all of the intelligence, artistic skills and adaption to habitat. They were represented on the skin by what looked like bendy barcodes (which I believe fade over time). Between the skin and the previous skin is where all the memories and emotions are stored. In a plasma-like substance so they are in suspension to form and be used in the energy generation process, which is one of the main purposes of our soul cell. The other is, of course, to create new life, at the point of the conception process.

When do we get a Soul?

Answer: I think it is clear when we get our Soul; it is at the point of conception. Within the womb there is a sea of passive Subatomic Soul Cells completely surrounding the sperm and egg. For the conception process to be completed at the very point that the sperm penetrates the egg, just one passive Subatomic Soul Cell is randomly selected to provide the "life force" of the new being and within that process the outer layer of the Subatomic Soul cell is ripped off and ingested into the new being, contributing information which will form the intelligence level of that individual. If it is a good fresh soul from say someone like "Einstein" then that being will be a genus of some kind, but the chances are much higher that the recipient will get an average run-of-the-mill Subatomic Soul Cell.

What also happens is that when the outer layer of the Subatomic Soul Cell is ripped off in the fusion of creating the new life, it become an active Subatomic Soul Cell and it starts to create the new life force that causes the cell to start to divide, and each time the cell splits, so does the Subatomic Soul divide, effectively giving each of the body's cells a subatomic soul cell (little battery) which are all directly connected to the central nervous system which will one day receive the final download, which will end that being's death.

What is the Life Force?

Answer: The Life-Force is the essence of the Soul's output. Its first and main function is to kick-start the life process at conception and then to maintain it throughout the life of that being, in turn creating new memories and emotions. The Life-Force is actually the output of the Subatomic Soul Cell generator which is powered by the downloaded memories and emotions of hundreds of previous beings, each one downloaded into each individual layer of the Subatomic Soul Cell which never gets any bigger. It merely compresses the layers and downloads into the same space so that each layer is pushed inward towards the core.

Where is the Life Force?

Answer: The location of the Life-Force is within the Subatomic Soul Cell. At the point of conception I believe there are three components, not two. We have the sperm, the egg, and the life force. At the precise point that the sperm penetrates the egg there is a nuclear reaction that splits the top surface off the soul cell which starts the life force in the new being and imparts the basis of intelligence into that being, thus forming the character and skill levels of that being.

What happens at the point of death?

Answer: For whatever reason our life is over, the end result is the same. The life force switches off once the download is completed and our body then instantly starts to decay. This is because the Subatomic Soul Cells have to be dispersed back into the environment to continue the cycle of life.

What is the white light in the tunnel experience?

Answer: At the point of death, just before brain death, there is the "download" process which takes all of the information from our brain and stores it in the Subatomic Soul Cell. The tunnel is the central nervous system and the connection between the body and the soul cell. During the download process the white light is a part of our conscience that is still functioning for a short time, and is still aware of going into that space within the atom. The "light" they are aware of is, I believe, the nucleus of the atom, which would appear like a star or the sun. And that is why NDE survivors say their life flashed before them. At that point they see everything that is being downloaded.

Will we see our loved ones again?

Answer: One of the main purposes of the Subatomic Soul Cell is to generate a continuing life force by what I believe is a physic or kinetic generator which is driven by the memories and emotions which are downloaded. Within these memories are all our loved ones and friends that have been part of our life, which will remain with us for eternity. I believe our memories and emotions are used in a continually running, non-stop movie, calling on all our life's experiences. Remember that energy cannot be destroyed. Even our memories are small electrical impulses of energy, and have an emotional weight which drives the life force generator. These precious memories of our family and friends will therefore be preserved which leaves every possibility that we may see our loved ones again.

Is there a Heaven & Hell? And where are they?

Answer: Within my theory, the answer is yes and no to these questions, and I say that because yes within the Subatomic Soul Cell, the storage area of all the emotions and memories could be regarded as heaven or hell location. However, for the soul cell to work it only requires variations of emotional states for the generation purpose to function, because, as previously mentioned it is the emotional weight of the soul layer that produces the energy by its variation of emotional weight of its layer in relationship to the adjoining layers. Personally I do not think that it requires evil emotions to function, as I feel that evil is a product of man's need to control his fellow man. Although initially I did think that each alternate layer could be good and evil to cause the generation process to function, but the more I applied the logic to the Subatomic Soul Cell process I felt that it would work with variation of emotions just as well. So Heaven Yes! Hell No! I hope I am right!

This "Heaven" would be constructed from all of the memories and emotions of the previous beings as described in the download process. These have been stored within the Soul Cell, so the thing we call Heaven is as if a play or film was being acted out using all those memories. Remember that these are little packets of energy and by them forming these story-like dreams which have the function of causing the generation process to work and thereby this could be described as a "Heaven State". But do we have a conscience state within that heaven? I believe that we do, and from Eden Alexander's experience of his NDE he said he did not know the being he was, which to me makes complete sense, but for me the thought of my memories going on providing energy for future life is good enough. After all, this is a logical explanation and as much as I would like to live in that dream state existence in the cycle of nature, we as individuals are insignificant in the greater scheme of things. To help you visualize what I am trying to describe, look at a DVD disc with its thousands of rings and imagine each ring is a previous being, and within each ring is the play area and the storage area. But now, instead of a flat disc, imagine a sphere with layers from beneath the skin right down to the core, maybe thousands of layers, and at the core a bright light

What is the human aura?

Answer: At the point of death, after the download and the Subatomic Soul Cells have been released to the environment, the body has given off between countless Subatomic Soul Cells and released them into the environment. The Cells have a "like charge" which are attracted to relatives of the deceased and this applies to all previous departed members of your family, going right back to the beginning of time, and all of these Subatomic Soul Cells stick like glue to form the human aura. This can also explain why people feel their departed relative are close This is because they sense in their brain the energy being emitted from the SSC.

How has intelligence advanced?

Answer: The Subatomic Soul Cell is a multi-purpose cell, and at the point of death when the "Download" process is performed, a skin or shell is formed around the Cell thus finalizing the life process of that being. However, during this part of the process a final download of additional things also takes place, whereby intelligence, artistic abilities, adaption to habitat are all then imbedded into the skin or shell and it is when this is complete that life ceases and decomposition begins in order to release the finalized Subatomic Soul Cell. It is a medical fact that at the instant of death, decomposition starts instantly at a cellular level. This is triggered by the finalization of the skin of the cell which breaks away the umbilical cord to allow the soul cells to be released to the environment to continue their journey to start the process all over again. So with the Soul Cell finalized it now ceases to be an active soul and becomes a passive soul cell, released to the environment just as with the pollen. The information on the skin will fade over time, but it will always impart that information required to start the life process and the basic cell construction when and if that soul cell is once again involved in that precise point of a conception process.

How do we get child prodigies?

Answer: As nature wants us to advance and increase our intelligence over time, this mechanism has a random element to the process and occasionally there are going to be lottery winners who get a fresh soul cell that was from a previously gifted individual. It is this random element of luck that results in the birth of child prodigies and the creation of geniuses like Albert Einstein and Stephen Hawkins.

How do clairvoyants "communicate" with the departed?

Answer: From the point of death, and after the download, the body starts to release the Subatomic

Soul Cells. These cells are released into the environment (initially from the surface of the skin) and scattered by the winds, like pollen, but because of the "like charge" of the Subatomic Soul Cell there is an attraction to the natural relatives of the deceased. When people who have lost someone and go to see a clairvoyant they have these Subatomic Soul Cells attached to them. These cells are functioning as generators and also emit or transmit a signal from the memories and emotions which are functioning within the top layer underneath the new skin. These emotions and memories are used in a random way to create a dream-like role play, and depending on the emotional weight of that role play will make the layer spin in a different direction to the adjoining level thus causing a kinetic or static charge. The emotions from this process give off an emission that is picked up by the clairvoyant, but this is not a two way communication. It is just as if they are picking up a radio type transmission, which is possible due to a heightened sensitivity to the very low signal. This is all speculation but it does give a feasible solution as to how clairvoyants do actually relay possible information from departed loved ones.

Why are we here?

Answer: I hope by now you will be able to answer that question for yourself. For me it is clear that we are here to produce memories and emotions to continually fuel the continuation of the life process within the Subatomic Soul Cell. The only question I have not been able to answer is; are we as individuals involved in the afterlife where our memories and emotions are going to be running? As much as I hope so, my deep feeling is once that download is complete we as individuals cease to exist. But maybe we don't and we walk in fields with fluffy clouds; unfortunately this part was not made available to me in my dream. But watching what was happening between each of the subatomic soul layers I knew there was a serenity emanating from them. So who know if what was there was someone's heaven. I would like to see it again. Death holds no fear for me and when I came close to taking my own life I was truly ready to go. The reason I was stopped was because I had not written this book and passed on the information which came to me in that dream. It was to make the human-race aware that religion is not the way. Just be true to yourself and treat people how you want to be treated and stop committing atrocities in the name of God.

Is there a God and where is his entity?

Answer: From my dream I had the feeling that yes there is a God but it is a part of the process rather than an entity. At the centre of every single Subatomic

Soul Cell is a core that is God, which means at the centre of every cell of our body is a God particle that is an essence of the life-force. This makes complete sense to me, rather than God being in heaven. Why shouldn't God and heaven be within us all? To me, this is a far more logical possibility.

The Conclusion:

I am very confident that my theory is sound as I feel there are no more-logical solutions on offer. I will indeed be surprised if my explanations are not confirmed and widely accepted in the not too, but what will it do to the world we live in? Religion would be shown for what it is. My hope is that it will make the world a much better place, with fewer wars and more kindness. Suicide bombers would be a thing of the past because there would be no promise of the 40 Virgins in paradise, but rather the realization that the consequences of their existence would be the basis of their eternity. But how many generations would it take for the radical religious fanatics to become extinct? Just imagine if my theory of the multi-layered subatomic soul cell is right and that each layer is packed with the total life experiences and emotions of each host going right back to the beginning of time, think what information and secrets would be revealed if we are eventually able to crack open a subatomic soul cell to a desired period. It would give us passive retro time travel, and just imagine how enlightening that we would be if we could be selective as to who's subatomic soul cell we could access!

Well if you want to experience the possibilities of this incredible world of the hypothetical Subatomic Soul Cell Theory, you can in the first of a series of fictional interpretations of my theory in an action-packed thriller that came to me while I was writing this book. It is the subject of a series of books, the first of which is entitled "The Soul Splitters - Episode One: The Swiss Time Code" in which James Bond meets Indiana Jones in a journey back in time to extract previously lost information by traveling in the subatomic inner-verse where all the answers are there for the picking. But as always there are those who would use this incredible resource for no good purposes. Will good overcome evil? Well, you will have to read the book to find out.

I hope you have enjoyed this, my first book about a very emotive subject. If you consider me to be a crackpot or insane, so be it. I have not written this book to try and persuade anyone; it has just been something I had to do. And as my fortunes in later life have dwindled, maybe if this book sells it will see me through to the time when I will also reach that final download. I know for me the thought of death no longer has any worries as I am convinced that at the point of my download I will continue to exist, as the reason for my being here has been fulfilled. I know I have more than adequately filled my memory banks, which will continue to give the life force for countless generation in the future!

Sadly, I am confident that if my subatomic Soul Cell System works, it would be equally possible for our consciousness to continue in the "dream state" of the

Subatomic Soul Cell generation process. Although our life's experience will continue to be fed into the Subatomic Soul Cell, the cell does not increase in size, so the layers are squeezed inwards to the centre, towards the God Particle where the memories that were us become at one with God!

So there you have it. I promised to answer the age-old questions and here is the one that has intrigued man since the beginning of time!

The cycle of the Subatomic soul cell

Its origin is in water (H_2O) which was delivered to Earth by comets.

a) It caused life on Earth to begin, starting with the single cell amoeba.

b) Through each generation of the subatomic soul cell it advanced in intelligence via the imprinted information on the skin of the cell.

c) It is the third component of the human conception process, providing the life force for each new being.

d) It provides the life force for the entire life of that being.

e) At the point of death it receives the download of that being's memories, emotions and intelligence.

f) When the download is complete the cell is "finalized" by the completion of the skin or shell, which is impregnated with the intelligence advancement package.

g) Via incineration or putrefaction the cells are released to the environment.